Best Wishes

Johny Callison

The Johnny Callison Story

JOHNNY CALLISON'S CAREER STATISTICS

Season Team	G	AB	R	H	2B	3B	HR	RBI	BB	SO	SB	Avg.
1958 Chicago (AL)	18	64	10	19	4	2	1	12	6	14	1	.297
1959 Chicago (AL)	49	104	12	18	3	0	3	12	13	20	0	.173
1960 Phillies	99	288	36	75	11	5	9	30	45	70	0	.260
1961 Phillies	138	455	74	121	20	11	9	47	69	76	10	.266
1962 Phillies	157	603	107	181	26	10	23	83	54	96	10	.300
1963 Phillies	157	626	96	178	36	11	26	78	50	111	8	.284
1964 Phillies	162	654	101	179	30	10	31	104	36	95	6	.274
1965 Phillies	160	619	93	162	25	16	32	101	57	117	6	.262
1966 Phillies	155	612	93	169	40	7	11	55	56	83	8	.276
1967 Phillies	149	556	62	145	30	5	14	64	55	63	6	.261
1968 Phillies	121	398	46	97	18	4	14	40	42	70	4	.244
1969 Phillies	134	495	66	131	29	5	16	64	49	73	2	.265
1970 Chicago (NL)	147	477	65	126	23	2	19	68	60	63	7	.264
1971 Chicago (NL)	103	290	27	61	12	1	8	38	36	55	2	.210
1972 New York (AL)	92	275	28	71	10	0	9	34	18	34	3	.258
1973 New York (AL)	45	136	10	24	4	0	1	10	4	24	1	.176
Career Totals	1886	6652	926	1757	321	89	226	840	650	1064	74	.264

The
Johnny Callison Story

John Wesley Callison
with
John Austin Sletten

VANTAGE PRESS
New York

FIRST EDITION

Published by Vantage Press, Inc.
516 West 34th Street, New York, New York 10001

Manufactured in the United States of America
ISBN: 0-533-09559-X

Library of Congress Catalog Card No.: 91-90872

1 2 3 4 5 6 7 8 9 0

John Wesley Callison: To my wife, Dianne, with love
John Austin Sletten: To my children, Kelly and Chad, Joseph, Daniel, and Christopher, with love

In Memoriam

Virgil Callison
Wilda Callison
Joy Lou Callison
Jerry Hammon
Ellen Jane (Focht) Sletten
Ole Sletten
Colonel Wallace Austin
Clara (Green) Austin
Richard Wade Lewis

With love to our family and friends

Johnny Callison
John Austin Sletten

Contents

Acknowledgments

A number of people deserve credit for making this book a possibility.

First of all, my family. My parents, Colonel and Mrs. Warren A. Sletten, provided me with the opportunity of an excellent education, giving me the love of reading, writing, and baseball. My brother, Rick, and sister, Chris, who have always kept their faith in me.

My son Joseph kept me company as I burned the midnight oil paging through scrapbooks and newspapers. My son Danny was always checking my progress and running errands for me. Christopher, my youngest son, maintained a keen interest: "How much money are we going to make doing this, Dad?" My son Chad helped me put together a synopsis to send to various publishers. And of course, to my daughter, Kelly, who is extra special to me.

My thanks to my mother-in-law, Martha Focht, and her friend, Sara Huff, for all the support and encouragement they've given me.

To all of these people, my family, I owe my greatest gratitude. Thanks for putting up with me and I love you.

Thanks to my friend, Susan Corr. She used her editorial acumen to edit the original manuscript. She put all the commas in the right places and sharpened my book considerably.

Thanks to Joe Hogan, a friend and great baseball fan, for spending time with me in thumbing through clippings and discussing opening ideas. Joe is a terrific writer and contributed significantly during the inception of this project.

I want to give special thanks to the Callison's daughters: Lori, Cindy, and Sherri. Their remarks are touching and come from the heart.

I want to thank, graciously, the many number of people I interviewed: Pete Callison, Don Jones, Helen Hammitt, Les Carpenter, Bobby Wine, Bobby Del Greco, Gene Mauch, Cookie Rojas, Dick Allen, and Clay Dalrymple. Their input was invaluable.

I would like to give a special thanks to Johnny's school friend, Don Jones. Don organized a meeting of Johnny's classmates and high school teammates in Bakersfield. Don made a two hour tape on which he captured the remarks of Richard Sanchez, Robert Carberry, Jerry Hammon and others. Their insight was humorous and appreciated.

Nancy Watkins and her husband, Don, have been long time friends of the Callisons. They put Johnny and me together. Thank you, Nancy and Don, for the connection and your candid remarks about the Callisons.

I also want to thank other special friends of the Callisons I interviewed. Joe and Gloria Skurla, Dottie and Melinda Delaney, Sam Ewing, Ken Kundler, and Mary Fitzgerald.

If it hadn't been for Michael Corbi, Johnny and I might still be trying to publish this book. Mike was my first source of support and encouragement, and gave me sound advise every step of the way. Thanks, Mike, for being our promoter.

Geri Dibiase, owner of Main Street Studio in Philadelphia, reproduced the pictures in the centerfold from old photographs and newspaper clippings. I recommend her highly.

Marsha Schwarz, a friend, who kept reading the book and giving me honest opinions and suggestions.

Personally, I would like to thank my nephew, Eric Leigh, for his interest in all of my endeavors. He wants to be a writer and should be encouraged from this project. Eric, you can do anything you want to do in life, if you're willing to put in the effort.

And without the great ballplayer, Johnny Callison, and his loving wife, there wouldn't be a story to tell. I met with Johnny and Dianne at their home in Glenside, Pennsylvania, once a month for nearly a year. Every experience was an enjoyable one as they candidly told me the accounts of their life. At first, of course, we were feeling each other out. But it wasn't long before we became comfortable with each other, and eventually we were advising each other about our own personal current events.

It is my hope that this book will touch you as it has the writer. The Callisons' story is much more than I thought it would be. It is a true trip down memory lane for those of us in the autumn of our years. Through its writing, I fulfilled a dream—that of being a major league baseball star through the times of my life. I thank the Callisons for that trip, and I hope the readers of this book enjoy a similar experience.

I love you, Johnny and Dianne. Thanks for the journey I once dreamed about!

—John Austin Sletten
April 14, 1991

Prologue

I don't know why I wanted to do it. Writing is a lot of work, and it often goes unrewarded. In fact, you're lucky if you can get your own family to read what you put down on hard copy.

Maybe it was suddenly an acute awareness of not liking what has happened to the game of professional baseball when I saw him standing there. Or, perhaps it was my own past as an addicted baseball fan who had spent so many of my waking hours listening, watching, and even scoring hundreds of baseball games. But here he was, Johnny Callison, standing next to me watching the Eagles and Bears battle in the fog on December 31, 1988.

Johnny Callison was the real thing. He played when there were sixteen teams in the majors. A time when each team had five or six good hitters, and three or four quality starting pitchers. A time we will never see again. These were "the boys of summer," guys that played the game because they loved it, not because they wanted to become instant millionaires for merely showing up.

I guess it was that, at first. I wanted to know what it was like to be a big leaguer in the golden era of baseball. What it was really like out there in those old, wonderful ballparks I'd pictured in my mind as a child, listening to baseball's "Game of the Day" on the radio, in a little town in Minnesota where I grew up. I needed to find out! So, I went in search of my dream. I wondered if I could live the experience through the words of Johnny Callison. And, I did!

It was one P.M. on June 21, 1989, when I left my office in Cherry Hill, New Jersey, to meet a two o'clock appointment at a restaurant called Tomatoes near Doylestown, Pennsylvania. I was somewhat apprehensive and nervous when I approached the Betsy Ross, which bridges New Jersey and Pennsylvania at the Delaware River. You see, I was en route to meet the day-time bartender of this eating and drinking establishment—Johnny Callison.

I'd been trying to contact Johnny for nearly six months. I had introduced myself to him that day when we were watching the Eagles game, but had left it at that, because I didn't want to bug him. I would have given anything to talk with him about baseball, but I knew it wasn't the right time.

A few days later I took out my baseball encyclopedia and did some quick research on Callison. I was immediately impressed with his career statistics and longevity in the major leagues. Also, I noticed he was born in Qualls, Oklahoma, which was not even listed on the map anymore. My curiosity became keen. I wondered how he had ever made it to the big leagues.

The next day I stopped by the Philadelphia Library to pull up July 7, 1964, from the *Philadelphia Inquirer*, which was stored on microfilm. I burned off three or four pages which gave me various accounts of the baseball all-star game played on that day at Shea Stadium, in Flushing, New York. On that particular day, Johnny Callison had hit a two-out home run to win the game for the National League in the bottom of the ninth inning. Again, I was impressed seeing his picture on those pages in the embrace of Willie Mays and Juan Marichal. At that moment, I really became enthusiastic about the project.

The next day I contacted a mutual friend, Nancy Watkins, and told her about my idea to write Johnny Callison's biography. She said Johnny was pretty shy and doubted he would let me delve into his life, but she'd ask. Nancy never called and four or five months passed. I was still determined, however, so I mailed Johnny a letter through the Philadelphia Phillies. Another month passed, and I heard nothing. By the first of June, I had pretty much given up on the idea. In mid June, I ran into Nancy at a graduation party. Much to my surprise, she approached me and gave me Callison's telephone number. "Call him," she said.

I was still reminiscing when I turned into the parking lot at Tomatoes. I had talked to Johnny a few days earlier, we had agreed to meet to talk about the book, at the restaurant. At first he told me, quite frankly, he really wasn't interested. Reticently, he finally agreed to at least listen to what I had to say. I took an outline of the book I'd prepared, slipped it in the vest pocket of my suit coat, and made my way toward the door of the restaurant.

I found the most remote corner of the bar, and when Johnny came over I introduced myself. The first thing he said was not encouraging: "John, I don't know about this book thing. Who would want to read a book about me?" he said with a confused look.

I replied convincingly, "I would!" Then, I ordered a beer, which made us both feel more comfortable.

Between customers, I spent three hours talking with Johnny. As he moved about the bar, I found myself watching him. He was friendly with everyone, and I sensed most of his customers were regulars. A couple of times he was handed a baseball, and he just autographed them like it was part of his job. During our short talks, he actually was giving me a lot of biographical information. In fact, after a couple of hours, I was getting the feeling he might really be interested in doing this biography. When it was time to leave, I asked, "Well, Johnny, shall we give it a shot?"

He smiled a sheepish grin, one I would get to know so well over the next year. "Okay, I'll do it! My wife and kids want me to do it, and they come first!"

We shook hands, and before I left he told me to call his wife, Dianne, the next day to arrange to pick up some articles from her which would get me started. The project had begun.

Nearly two years have passed since that day, during which time I have lived "The Johnny Callison Story." I did fulfill my dream, perhaps I became Johnny Callison during the writing of his story. It's a wonderful story of the American dream come true, and it's more than just a baseball book. It's a story of a young man coming from the humblest, most difficult beginnings reaching the top of sports celebrity through dedicated hard work and determination.

It is not simply the story of a young boy growing up fulfilling his dreams by achieving his goal of becoming a big league ballplayer. It is more than that. It is about a family and their life through the obstreperous "sixties." What makes the story exceptional is not that they were a major league baseball family, rather, it is their pursuit of a life bolstered by love and support.

Many young American boys dream of playing major league baseball. I know I did! Johnny Callison fulfilled that dream before his twentieth birthday. In the years that followed, Johnny became a symbol for millions not only as a baseball player, but as a down to earth, caring human being who put family first. The third child of a poverty stricken family—he went on to hit 226 career home runs, and was a premier fielder with a powerful arm.

From the hot streets of East Bakersfield, to 16 years in the major leagues, during which time he played for four major league clubs, the White Sox, Phillies, Cubs, and Yankees, the name Callison became a household word. But, it wasn't as simple and glorious as one might suspect.

Here, then, is Johnny Callison's true story: the candid answers to the questions that his fans have been asking for nearly twenty years. WHERE DID YOU COME FROM—WHERE DID YOU GO, JOHNNY CALLISON? The book abounds with those memories of his playing days when it was "Callison for President" in Philadelphia. The book movingly recounts the private events of his personal life from the humblest of beginnings to his personal triumphs and letdowns in and out of baseball. Brimming with the nostalgia and detail that baseball fans love, *The Johnny Callison Story* is an affectionate self-portrait of a true American hero.

On a personal note, during the past two years, I've spent a lot of time with the Callisons. They are the real thing! Johnny and

Dianne have been married for nearly thirty-four years—they're still crazy about each other. They are loving parents and good, honest, decent people. It was thrill to me just to meet them, and writing their book has been an exciting experience. If ever a story should be told, it is the Callisons'.

In a world now raging with war in Saudi Arabia, and the filthy drug culture that penetrates our country; it's been a pleasure to backtrack a bit to the way things once were. So, take a ride with me to 21st and Lehigh on the "El." Back to a time when a box seat was $3.25, a reserved seat $2.25, general attendance $1.50, and a bleacher seat $.75, and a zip top can of Ortlieb beer was the greatest thing of all—$.40. Coca-Cola was $.40, a hoagie $.50, cigarettes $.40, and, of course, that baseball game necessity—Cracker Jack was a quarter. And, as Richie Ashburn would say, "There was that Johnny Callison!"

—John Austin Sletten
February 19, 1991

The Johnny Callison Story

Chapter One

Calypso of Bakersfield

*Highway 66 is the main migrant road. 66—the long concrete path across
the country, waving gently up and down on the map, from the Mississippi
to BAKERSFIELD—over the red lands and the gray lands, twisting up into
the mountains, crossing the Divide and down into the bright and terrible
desert, and across the desert to the mountains again, and into the rich
California valleys. 66 is the path of a people in flight, refugees from dust
and shrinking land, from the thunder of tractors and shrinking ownership,
from the desert's slow northward invasion, from the twisting winds that
howl up out of Texas, from the floods that bring no richness to the land and
steal what little richness is there. From all of these the people are in flight,
and they come into 66 from the tributary side roads, from the wagon tracks
and the rutted country roads. 66 is the mother road, the road of flight.*
                                    —John Steinbeck, *The Grapes of Wrath*

Comiskey Park
Chicago, Illinois
September 10, 1958

For a moment, I feel that life is rivaling my dreams, as I stand
there swinging a handful of bats, with my spikes gripping the
dirt of the on-deck circle. Suddenly, I feel as if I am involved in
a rich man's game: my spikes feeling light as feathers, the
tailored uniform fitting me like a glove, and my fielder's mitt

1

lying on the bench in the enclosed dugout—it cost more than my father could once earn in a week.

I peer into the distance at deep center field, fixing my eyes on the Longines clock which is situated directly above the huge electric scoreboard. My attention is drawn to two words which are encircled within the facsimile of a baseball: A HIT. Just below and to the left, it reads in letters seemingly a mile high: ALWAYS BY CHESTERFIELD.

I could use a cigarette about now, I think, as I whip the three bats around two or three times and then discard one with my last swing as I drop down to one knee. *Oh God, how I want a hit right now*, I'm thinking. *This would be my first at bat in the Big Show.* I look into center field at the clock again and realize that it was less than four hours ago that we'd arrived here at 35th and Shields on Chicago's South Side.

I had just been brought up from Indianapolis, where I'd completed my first season in Triple A ball. I had led the American Association in home runs with 29 and batted .283, which was not too shabby after a slow start, 93 runs batted in and a more dubious honor of being the strikeout king of the American Association with more than 120. *But I guess nobody worries more than me*, I'm thinking as I stand up, take three or four swings, and discard another bat, dropping to one knee again in the on-deck circle.

I look around the stadium, remembering the sign that hovers over the six entrances at the front of the ballpark: COMISKEY PARK . . . HOME OF THE WHITE SOX. I had never seen a major league ballpark before, and now I'm playing in one. Frank Sullivan is pitching for the Boston Red Sox, and I begin concentrating on his throwing again to look for that certain hitch or motion that will signal a fastball. I know I can hit anybody's fastball—but wait a minute—not too fast!

Anyway, my mind is racing too fast now, and I can't really concentrate on Frank Sullivan. Instead my eyes take me to home plate, and I begin admiring the adroit workmanship of the groundskeepers with the chalking of the rectangular batter's boxes.

From there I track the chalk down the right-field line, and I can't help but notice how the foul territory, which is so vast between home plate and first base, begins to narrow quickly once past the infield cutout to the right-field corner, where the distance reads 352. My eyes drift slightly to the left, and there is Jackie Jensen slapping the pocket of his glove. My eyes come back to home plate, and I start following the chalk line past Frank Malzone at third to the 352 mark in the left-field corner. My eyes move to the right, and there stands my childhood hero, Ted Williams. Old number 9 bats left and throws right, just like me—or I should say more correctly—I like him. Ironically, I'm wearing number 9 myself. *Wow! It couldn't get any better than this*, I think. I wonder what Ted Williams will think of my first at bat? Then, I look farther to the right where a five- or six-foot metal fence cuts across, connecting deep left center with deep right center, forming the center-field fence. Just beyond the fence are the bullpens, and it was 400 feet out there. I wonder if I will ever juice one into those bullpens. I know I can— and there in front of the center-field fence is Jimmy Piersall in the ready position.

I take another practice swing and then look at the concrete and steel one more time, noticing its perfect symmetry—even the eight arc lights that sit on top of the second deck seem absolutely strategically placed. The stadium has two covered decks all the way around, and only in that spot in dead center field, where the electric scoreboard and bullpens are, remains uncovered. Yes, it is like a dream, but now it is time. Then, suddenly, everything seems the same, yet different, and the thrill of pride is surging ahead of my blood through my veins with the tiny current of fear that I won't quite make it.

Bust as far back as I can remember, baseball was the test that I always passed. It was always right for me, and I can remember the early years with pleasure, sensual pleasure, sun, wind, earth, leather, horsehide, the drone of insects, water that chased the thirst, and the incomparable sounds of a ball being hit, or hitting the pocket of a glove. The broken bat that had been salvaged with a small nail and white tape; the old brown balls that had been literally separated from their covers; and playing from morning until dusk softened the light of the summer sky.

At first there was no thought, just sheer fun, a bunch of kids choosing sides. If we had five kids, two would be at bat and three in the field. You would stay at bat until you made out, and then you went to the outfield and that guy went to the infield, and the infielder became the pitcher and the pitcher became a batter. We called this game "work-up," and the best batters were always up and I could always hit the best. Numbers of kids never mattered; if we had twenty kids there would be ten positions, and for rules there was anarchy and argument.

There was an art to choosing sides. It was done with a bat. One kid tossed the bat to another, and each would exchange grips, going from the barrel up to the handle until crunch time, and that was the "eagle's claw" at the knob of the bat. The kid who gripped the end of the bat with an "eagle's claw" had the right to the first pick. I was always the first one picked for any team, so I never bothered with the bat routine. I was just happy with the fact of being the first one chosen.

"I take the Okie," the winner declared, meaning me. I would have preferred "Johnny," but "Okie" was where it settled and the nickname fit. I was the only white boy, and I had come to Bakersfield from Cherokee County, Oklahoma, with my mother, brother, and two sisters on a train in 1944 when I was only five years old. Actually, the expression "Okie" meant trash out in Bakersfield at the time, but the kids didn't think of me in that way—they were using the name in jest. So, the name did not go away and I got used to it.

My reminiscing has to end now as the public address system rings out: "NOW BATTING FOR THE WHITE SOX—NUMBER NINE—JOHNNY CALLISON."

*　　*　　*

4

Pete Callison:

We've been pretty proud of Johnny, you know; it's something no one else around here has ever done. We came to Bakersfield in 1944 during the war. My dad, Virgil, was overseas with a quartermaster corps, and about the time we came out here he was in on the landing at Normandy. My mother, Wilda, had a sister and a stepsister who had settled in Bakersfield, and they had made some arrangement for her to purchase a house there for $1,300 cash. I guess you could say that we were the tail end of the great migration from the dust bowl and the depression—with little alternative we moved to Bakersfield, California, the land of golden opportunity and wartime jobs.

My two sisters, Joy Lu and Judith Ann, Johnny, and I were born in a place called Qualls, Oklahoma. Don't bother to look it up, it's not even there anymore. However, if you look at a map of Oklahoma you'll find Cherokee County in the northeast quadrant of the state. Talequah is the county seat and Qualls was about eighteen miles out in a place called the Cookston hills. It's mountainous back in there, and I remember my cousin always calling my dad the Cookston hillbilly because he came from there, somewhere near a little hamlet called Gore. Dad's folks were from the Gore area and our Mom was more near Qualls. Mom and Dad had a difficult time making money around there, as did everyone else in the mid- and late thirties. When Johnny was just learning to walk they worked at a place called the Woodlawn Dairy near Talequah. Mom and Dad milked cows, churned butter, and anything else that needed to be done around the farm.

We moved to my uncle's dairy farm for a while near Broken Arrow, Oklahoma. We lived at Fort Gibson, which was very near my uncle's farm where they worked. Once in a while we would take a train trip to Talequah to visit our grandfather Wesley Callison's place. These trips were a big deal for us because Talequah had a movie theater and my older sister Joy Lu and I would take Johnny to the movies. He'd always take turns sitting on our laps so we wouldn't have to pay for him.

We moved from Fort Gibson to Tulsa for a short time and then to a place in Gore by my dad's folks. We lived in a little old place off the main street above a store—Joy Lu and I went to school there; but it wasn't long before we moved to a smaller place just outside of town, and I remember it being pretty cold there in the evenings. Somewhere around that time Dad went off to war, leaving Mom with the four of us; she was always like a rock that kept us going. We still have some pictures of Dad in his uniform holding Johnny, but he, of course, was too young to remember Dad when he first left for military duty.

Naturally, things seemed to get worse for us after Dad left because Mom had to do even more work to make ends meet. Soon, we moved to a house in Talequah. Yeah, it was a small house at 598 North Muskogee Avenue on the corner of Goingsnake Street. How about that for an intersection? We lived right on a creek, and Johnny and I played there all the time together. Directly across from our house was an Indian college—Johnny and I would run around over there a lot, too, just for something to do. Funny, I was back that way a few years ago and that college is still there and operating—Northeastern State College.

Johnny and I slept in one bedroom, and I got a good case of poison ivy one time when the vine grew right in through our bedroom window. Johnny stepped on a rattlesnake once, and he was very fond of a large St. Bernard dog that would come around every day. There isn't much more to say about the place other than what I have just said—we were really poor and just tried to make the best of the situation—although it is the first address I ever remember, so it must have been better than some of the other places we holed up in.

It was sometime around that time when our grandfather John Icem Faddis, our mother's father, passed away. I remember Johnny sitting on his knee when he churned butter, and when he died Johnny was there in the room with the rest of us. In fact, back in those days, if someone died with their eyes open, they covered the

Bakersfield was something alright! Farms, oil derricks, and factories lay next to each other all over the San Joaquin Valley. They were growing cotton, alfalfa, and there were a lot of fruit growers too. I remember steel works, iron foundries, and factories for cotton goods. Bakersfield produced a lot of bedding goods in those days, so you had quite a mix of people: landowners, businessmen, and oil barons. There was a great deal of money around, and this made it even tougher to be so poor. Even as a kid I could see the difference, and it made me an unhappy and quiet kid. When I was in school it must have been pretty noticeable. I was no great shakes as a student, but I kept quiet and the teachers treated me extra nice, it seemed, probably because they felt sorry for me.

My fifth-grade teacher, Mrs. Hammitt, seemed to take an immediate liking to me. She used to marvel at the way I played ball on the playground. She told me right off that I was the best ballplayer she'd ever seen at my age. It seemed like she always paid special attention to me, whether it was helping me with my school lessons or making certain I wasn't hungry. She got me interested in the newly formed Junior Baseball Association. But I was reticent to play because I didn't have a glove or spikes. Upon such advisement, she took me to a sporting goods store and bought me both. I'll never forget that day and I tried to say thank you, but I didn't do that very well, either. She said not to worry. The glove and the spikes were an investment in my future, and someday, when I was playing for the Chicago Cubs (they were originally from Chicago), she would ask me to get her tickets for a game.

Before I got my glove and spikes I would always have to borrow a glove—I didn't worry about the spikes as I looked at them as a luxury item. On Sundays I would stand in the vacant lot next to the Catholic church and wait for mass to end. I played for a team of boys about my own age and we would play against a team of grown-up men every Sunday afternoon. This was a serious game played with white balls and real bases. I was the big clean-up hitter for my team, and we would generally win the game because the men would be falling down drunk by the seventh inning. It seemed everyone in the neighborhood would show up to watch these games, and sometimes I'd feel pretty important.

So, when I got my new glove and spikes, I first started to play organized ball in the Junior Baseball Association. Our coach, Jim Boone, who'd played in the Negro Professional League, made me a third baseman because I had the strongest arm on the team, and sometimes I would pitch. Boone had been a third baseman, and he taught me the fundamentals of the position and the whole game. He knew his baseball and provided me with a wealth of baseball wisdom for that time. His own kid played for our team, too, and he was the catcher. Boone was serious about this baseball and made us toe the mark. I would stay at his house overnight before a game so he could keep an eye on us and we would be ready for the game the next day.

Through Boone's tutelage and some God-given natural ability, I received a trophy as the JBA's outstanding participant of 1953 at Sam Lynn Park. The next day my picture was in the *Californian*—that was a big deal for me at the time. But then Boone was gone. His wife shot him dead as a doornail and I never knew why. Jim Boone was a good guy—he was my friend and he took a special interest in me. He helped a lot of other kids as well, and I couldn't understand why that would happen to a nice man like Boone. However, trouble must have followed him through life because he had told me once that he had been kicked out of East St. Louis for some reason or another.

I guess, without realizing it, I was becoming special around Bakersfield. Everyone knew me and liked me because I was a good ballplayer. For the most part, I played with the Mexican and black kids, but then as the years passed, most of them went to work in the fields and factories and I went on to East Bakersfield High School, feeling very much like a fish out of water. It was the same old problem, and I was becoming even more sensitive as I got older. I dressed like hell and I did not have a car. I had acquired a new interest—girls—but I was afraid to ask any of them out. You couldn't take a date on a bus and that was my only means of travel. Once, a so-called friend of mine who had a car set up a double date with me, but for some reason or another he did not show up and I had to cancel my date. I felt inadequate once again.

Things were getting worse at home. My brother, Pete, joined the navy, and it seemed like Dad was drinking more than ever. I forced myself to go home at night; I'd only go home when I knew my mother would be there, which was usually around 10:00 P.M. as she worked unusual hours in order to keep the family financially secure enough to meet the bare necessities. In fact, I really couldn't take it anymore, and I decided to quit school and join the navy myself. Well, I ran away for a day or two—not too far, because my mother found me and talked me into coming back.

I was playing high school ball, and my coach—a wonderful man, Les Carpenter—told me he thought I had the talent to be a big leaguer if I'd work hard with him and stay in school. He was a major influence in my life, and he worked hard to make me a complete ballplayer who could use his noggin on the field. This sure came in handy later when I was a teenage phenom in the Bigs. He switched me to the outfield and I was more comfortable there. I was never crazy about the hot corner with all those rocks and pebbles waiting to skew the hard ball off your head or between the legs. He taught me to slide well, too. I couldn't believe when I started playing professional ball how few of the big leaguers could slide well. He also became a valuable friend who kept me from throwing away my baseball career before it even began. And, as if all that was not enough, he fed me. He brought me to his house for lunch and invited me to delicious evening barbecues where I got to eat really great food and meet nice people.

Then, in a dramatic way, Mrs. Hammitt came back into my life. She kept track of me, and when I told her about running away, she simply said that if I ever wanted to do it again to come see her and she would take care of me. Subsequently, I ran into a scrape with the law and got arrested with some other kids for stealing hubcaps. I hadn't stolen any but I was there. Well, Mrs. Hammitt came to my rescue and I wound up moving in with them in my junior year of high school.

I hated leaving my mother, but she just seemed to understand—she was a wonderful mother. She had to work all the time to try make ends meet, and with my old man hanging around the house drinking all the time, I simply did not want to be there. So, moving in with the Hammitts and their two adopted children marked a new beginning for me. They helped me organize myself and set up schedules for doing homework. They forced me to look at life as something to embrace rather than run away from. They even helped me buy a car, realizing it was a necessary evil because they lived across town from East Bakersfield High and it was a long ways to walk.

Life was getting better, and it was because of the special people who were good enough to help me. I was playing baseball, football, and basketball—I excelled in every sport and found my name appearing in the paper seemingly every day. I wasn't that big, but I could throw, hit, kick, and run over and around anyone that would get in my way. I was a fierce competitor and I wanted to be the best. I played ball year round, and it was my baseball playing that seemed to be attracting most of the attention. Baseball scouts were appearing out of the woodwork, and the idea of being a big leaguer was starting to settle in my head.

*   *   *

Helen Hammitt:

I first met Johnny when he arrived in my fifth-grade class in elementary school. He always had a pleasant smile and was a well-behaved student, but was in the lower part of his class academically. I did a little investigating and found out he had very little support from home. He'd come to school hungry sometimes, and I would see that he would get something more substantial to eat. I noticed right off that he was very strong physically, and at the age of ten he was exceptional in all sports. I always said he could run faster backwards than any of the other kids could run forward.

My husband and I liked to go on short trips over the weekends, and we would try to take Johnny and his friend Richard Sanchez as often as they were allowed to go with us. Sometimes Johnny's younger sister, Judy Ann, would go with us as well. We took Johnny to see the ocean for the first time and to Sequoia National Park where we liked to go camping. I can still picture him sledding in the mountains where he first saw snow. You know, right from the start Johnny always seemed to be part of our family. I tried to encourage him because he seemed to need a lot of help in different ways due to the fact he didn't get much attention from his family and even from some of the other teachers. I guess he thought I was going out of my way, but I wasn't—it was just my way, and happy children give me my biggest source of energy. When Johnny received the help he needed in school he did just fine—it wasn't that he wasn't smart. It was just his situation. We picked up on his athletic ability right away and encouraged him to use his talents. We attended practically every game he played, from JBA through high school, and enjoyed his success immensely.

As far as his parents are concerned, I can't really say much about them because I didn't know them very well. Johnny had a real good mother—she was really a strong person who always tried to make everything right for her family. I really felt sorry for her. Johnny's father had an alcohol problem and I saw the results of that sometimes at a ball game. He'd sit in the crowd and yell the most awful things: "Johnny, hit that ball or I'll hit you!" We were horrified at some of the things his dad would say. He had a way of pressuring Johnny that was not very kind.

I think Johnny's mother was relieved when he came to live with us. She was really something to sacrifice her own feelings for the well-being of her son. He had just run away from home when I first presented him with the idea of coming to live with our family. I told him that the next time he wanted to run away, he should run away to our place. My remark must have sunk in because it was not too long after that when Johnny came to tell me that his dad had gathered up all the Christmas presents, tossed the packages in the backyard, and set the gifts on fire. He was quite upset about that, as anyone, of course, would be. We did some negotiating back and forth, and Johnny came to live with us not too long afterwards.

Johnny seemed relieved when he came; however, it took awhile for him to become adjusted to our way of living. He wasn't used to doing homework because he never went home until his mother came in from work, which was around nine or ten o'clock in the evening. He waited until then because he didn't want to be home alone with his dad. When Johnny came to live with us he was quick to notice that our children did their homework immediately after dinner. Shortly thereafter, he started coming home with some books, and from then on he did his assignments, too.

Athletically, Johnny excelled. He enjoyed football and we really enjoyed watching him play football. He could really dodge around, and I remember this one game when we were going to play Taft (a big rival). They had a really big fellow, and the papers talked about this player stopping Johnny. Well, Johnny practically ran between his legs. He was just different from the other kids in sports, and from the very beginning he was simply exceptional.

During that first summer with us Johnny got a job in the country. He also was dating Dianne. We had considered switching schools because the one he was attending was way across town; however, a better alternative seemed to help him get a car. We purchased a car for him, and each week when he received his paycheck he would sign it over to us to repay the car loan and we'd give him back some spending money. He appreciated our help, and we felt we had made the right decision. It would have been an awful thing for him to have left his school for another. He was so well known at East for his athletics and Dianne was becoming an important part of his life. Dianne was a good match for Johnny; she was such a nice girl, and we just hoped that it would work out between them. I thought he was pretty lucky to have found her. She came from a nice home and was one of four girls in the family. I was always really fond of her and I know Johnny was, too.

Although I was disappointed, he signed with the White Sox and not the Cubs; I can still picture the day that he left for his first spring training. He said to me, "Imagine being paid all this money and then doing the thing that you like to do best." I could only smile outwardly and more so inwardly! And wouldn't you know it, later in his career he did wear that Cub uniform. I thought, *Now, isn't that just like Johnny; he never forgot anyone that was good to him.* Looking back, Johnny and I came to appreciate each other.

*   *   *

Excited, nervous? Oh no, not me! Early Wynn struck out, retiring the side, and I stole second base. Feeling somewhat chagrined when I realized there were three outs, I picked myself up out of the dust and made my way toward left field as Aparicio tossed me my glove. En route to my position I began thinking that Daley, the Red Sox catcher, must have been unaware of the third out, too, because he made the throw, and Don Buddin, the shortstop, surely tried to put the tag on. I felt better until I assumed my position and felt my knees shaking so badly—I kept saying to myself, *Please, don't hit me a fly ball, please, don't hit me a fly ball. I'll never be able to catch it.* It was worse than that feeling I had before a football game, with butterflies in my stomach and wondering how big number 86 over there really was. But 86 was never that tough, and now it was the third inning and I still had the jitters. Perhaps it was because baseball is a more complex game. Football is more of a team sport, where with baseball, while collectively it is a team effort, you are alone when it's your time at bat or when a screaming line drive is shooting at you! In baseball you're always on the spot and I never felt more on the spot then I did on this, my debut in the big leagues.

My legs felt weak as I pounded the pocket of my glove while Early Wynn took the last of his warm-up pitches. I looked down the left-field line toward the home plate area stands, trying to spot where Dianne and my daughter, Lori, were seated. I wondered how Dianne and Lori were doing. Our daughter would soon be one year old, and it was hard to believe she was already at a major league ball game. Then it hit me. It was the first major league game I was ever at as well, and I was playing in it. Suddenly, I realized how quickly my career was moving—it was like the male version story of Cinderella and I was afraid I was going to turn into a pumpkin real soon.

*   *   *

Dianne Callison:

We had put nearly everything we owned in the car and had driven to Chicago from Indianapolis that very day. The White Sox had secured a room for us at the Piccadilly Hotel on the South Side near the ballpark. We had no more than checked in when Johnny had to leave for the stadium. I, of course, took Lori with me to the game. When I'd settled the two of us in our seats, I remember just looking around, thinking how cavernous the whole place seemed. When I saw Johnny's name in the lineup and watched him run out to left field I could hardly believe my eyes—I was so proud of him.

I first remember noticing Johnny when he seemed to be paying particular attention to me in the seventh grade. I didn't like him—you know how you are when you are kids. I just didn't like him. Then, one day he tried to follow me home from school and I didn't like that at all. While he was still at a distance I picked up a bamboo pole, and when he approached me I hit him with it, saying, "Don't you ever follow me home again!"

Well, looking back at things, I really can't say why I did such a thing, but I give him credit for his persistence, although we didn't

18

form a relationship until our junior year in high school. I ran into him at the county fair and he told me he needed a ride home. My girlfriend Merna had a car that night and we had come to the fair together with one other girlfriend. I asked Merna if it would be alright if we gave Johnny Callison a ride home, and she reticently told me it would be alright. Everyone knew about Johnny's athletic prowess, and, I must admit, his terrific ability intrigued me more than a bit.

He and I wound up in the backseat that night, and for some reason I allowed him to work his way into a position to kiss me. I guess it was that first kiss—*Wow! I really like this guy.* Just before we dropped him off he asked me to go out with him, and I played it cool. But I was ecstatic when he called the next week, asking to go out on a double date with him and two other classmates. On the night of the scheduled date, after I was ready to go, he called me on the telephone to inform me the other guy couldn't get his father's car and he'd have to cancel the date. I was simply furious and felt as though I'd been stood up.

A week or two later he came up to me at a school dance and asked me out again. I told him I was annoyed with him because I felt he had stood me up. He then began to explain to me that it wasn't his fault because he didn't have a car and was forced to rely on his friend for transportation that evening. He told me, "I really want to take you out." I said, "Sure you do," and I walked away. But it wasn't long after when I went to one of our high school football games in which, of course, Johnny had been the star player and I had paid particular attention to him. I remember it was in Portersville, and when the game was over Johnny came running toward me as I waited and hoped this time that he would ask me out. Even though I was going steady at the time, I had it in my head that I would like to have a date with him. Sure enough, he asked me for a date and I accepted, knowing the possible consequences as I was going steady.

Suddenly, with the crack of a bat, my reverie was over. I was in Chicago, Illinois, ready to watch my husband, Johnny, play in his first major league baseball game. Our daughter, Lori, was by my side. We'd come a long way in a few short years. And, perhaps, I was more nervous than he for the moment.

*　　*　　*

I didn't get that fly ball hit to me in the third inning, and when I came up in the fourth I just kept telling myself, *Don't strike out. Don't strike out.* But as I took this at bat I began feeling calmer because it just didn't seem Sullivan was throwing as hard as I thought he would. When he came in with another fastball I belted it up into the wind in right center field, where it fell for a double. My God, I'd hit a double in my first official at bat, windblown or not; I was more than surprised. My teammates, however, left me stranded and the rains came, delaying the game for thirty-two minutes as we trailed the Red Sox 1–0, leaving the game not yet official. During the delay I smoked one cigarette after another and just hoped that the contest would resume so my hit wouldn't be stricken from the record. After the tarp was removed from the field I assumed my position in left field, a position I hadn't played all year, when I quickly received my first opportunity in the field. I heard the crack of the bat and saw the ball heading my direction. It was a towering fly ball which I circled under and made the catch without a problem—another milestone.

I was still smoking cigarettes in the dugout, one after the other, when I came up in the sixth inning. Sullivan threw me another fastball and I ripped it on a line into left center field. Earl Torgerson had opened the sixth with a single and then Jim Landis had walked, so when I hit my shot Torgy scored and I not only had my second consecutive double but I had my first RBI. Early Wynn was next, and he singled Landis and me home, giving me my first run scored. Wow! This was becoming too much. The big leagues couldn't be this easy! In the eighth inning I came up again to face the Red Sox's relief pitcher, Bud Byerly. He threw me a change-up, and I slapped it into left center for a single to get another scoring situation going. But much to my surprise and relief, Al Lopez sent Jim Rivera in to pinch run for me. The fans booed when they took me out of the game, and I was even more bewildered. But it had been a perfect debut—certainly a dream come true!

*   *   *

Don Jones:

Johnny Callison is a legend around these parts. When anyone talks about great athletes they either mention Johnny or Frank Gifford first. Frank played for Bakersfield College, where I attended school, and of course, Johnny went to big leagues right out of high school.

You know, I saw Johnny perform some baseball feats that I didn't think were possible. Some of them were difficult to believe. In fact, I wouldn't have believed some of what he did with a bat if I hadn't seen it with my own eyes. Even after witnessing what he did it was difficult to believe he'd done it.

There was a girls' gymnasium beyond the right-field fence near our high school, and it was a batter's dream to try and hit the ball off that structure. Well, I saw Johnny, at least once and I think twice, hit a ball completely over the top of that building. In fact, I watched the ball bounce on the road behind the gymnasium when it came out of orbit. He hit those shots well over four hundred feet. All of us that were there thought those rockets Johnny launched would have sailed out of Yankee Stadium. I remember just being amazed—I saw it but I didn't believe it!

I was a catcher, and one day Johnny was taking batting practice when he turned around and said, "Don, look at this."

I responded, "Look at what?" wondering what was next.

"Watch the ball when I hit it—I'm going to hit it so square that it will take off the bat like a knuckleball," he replied. Sure enough, when the next pitch came in he smacked it out toward second base and the ball didn't spin at all. He did it several other times as the whole team watched the exhibition. We all saw it but we couldn't believe it!

Another story I like to tell is when I was playing baseball at Bakersfield College. For some reason the baseball field was laid out on an incline, with home plate the low point and everything else going uphill. It was great for the outfielders but hell on a hitter, especially a power hitter. Rumor pretty much had it that no one could ever hit a home run out of our ballpark. Well, Johnny played in Bakersfield in Class C ball right out of high school, and he happened by when we were practicing that following spring—probably just before he went to his first spring training. I must have told him about this ballpark and that no one could ever hit one over the fence because a batter had to hit uphill. He calmly picked out a bat, strolled up to the plate, and smacked the first four or five pitches cleanly over the right- and center-field fences. I saw it, my teammates saw it, and our coaches saw it. None of us believed it—how could you?

Yeah, Johnny and I ran around together. I first met him when we were playing in the Junior Baseball Association. We were on different teams then, but we got to know each other and became pals. Johnny was always on the shy side and didn't say too much, but he was always there with that grin on his face. Often, I wondered what he was thinking. I knew if I'd ask him he'd just shrug his shoulders and smile again. He was a good guy and always a real true friend.

When Johnny spoke he usually did it with his bat. When he would hit a ball it would just seem to explode off the bat. We all noticed his special abilities right off—way, way back in JBA. Sometimes, when he wasn't around, we'd talk about Johnny making the big leagues. He just had that edge and it wasn't a razor's edge. I was always about the same size as Johnny and could never figure out why I couldn't do the things he could. I mean, there wasn't one thing he couldn't do better than me athletically. He used to tell me that he could walk faster than I could run. He was kidding, of course, but I wasn't so sure that he couldn't walk faster than I could run.

I was a competitor and used to try to figure out something I could beat him at, and one time I thought I'd solved the situation. I had a Ping-Pong table, and I invited him to the house to lure him into a game I was sure he'd never played before. I'd been practicing, thinking I was pretty good at the sport. Johnny came over and I took him out back to the table. He picked up a paddle, got the feel of it, and we vollied back and forth for a few minutes while I explained the rules of the game to him. Okay, I'm getting anxious, and we started a game. I was quickly up eight or nine points—it was thirteen to five, something like that, and I'm getting a feeling that I might win this contest. Wrong again! About this time Johnny had figured out the game—it never took him too long—and he scored fifteen or sixteen unanswered points to win. I was pissed off but I didn't let him know it. I never invited him to play Ping-Pong again, either.

In high school Johnny and I played ball together on the same team. We played high school sports, football and baseball (he played basketball and I didn't), and we played baseball all summer whether it was legion, semipro ball, or just a pickup game. I was a pretty good ballplayer, as were several of us on our teams, but compared to Johnny we were nothing. In all the tough games we played we'd just try to hang in the game until we could get Johnny into a situation to win it for us. For instance, if a game was tight going into the latter innings, someone would invariably get on base and here comes Johnny. We could all relax then because that is the way he played the game. We knew he'd win it for us—it would be just a matter of how he was going to do it this time. He'd come up to the plate just as carefree as if he were going to a movie—I'm telling you he intimidated the opposing pitchers. Sometimes, if a pitcher was having a good day, he might get a couple of strikes on him, then—*bang!!* He'd hit a home run, triple, double, or do something that might happen to the rest of us once in a lifetime. We'd see it and we couldn't believe it!

Johnny wasn't big in stature but he was all power—he had power all over him. He had those Popeye-type forearms and huge, huge hands. He'd lash at the ball like Zorro snapped a whip, and he also had very strong legs, which gave him lightning-type speed.

Johnny was the tailback on our football team and I was a guard. We ran from the old single-wing formation and sometimes I'd pull and get out in front of him—he'd usually push me where he wanted me to go, and his shove seem to give me thirty-five or forty pounds more thrust. He was tremendously strong and I always marveled at the momentum generated from such a small frame—he just had trigger-action reflexes! But it was his speed that always impressed me—that incredible speed! Incredible speed!

I like to tell about this one game in high school. I had singled, and it was one of those situations I'd described above. We'd worked a close game up to the point where Johnny could win it for us. I'm leading off first base and Johnny rips a ball way the hell out in right center field over everyone's head. I'm running as fast as I can go and somewhere between second and third I hear Johnny: "Don, get out of my way. Get out of my way!" I can't believe it—I'm halfway to second base when he leaves home plate, and now he's dogging me between second and third, telling me to get the hell out of the way. Speed, yeah, that was some speed, and believe me, I was running as fast as I could. I guess if he'd walked we would have gotten to home plate about the same time.

Johnny was something else, and every once in a while I'll meet with some of the old guys, you know, and we'll talk and agree that he was the best athlete any of us have ever seen. I've known Dianne, his wife, since the fourth grade, way before Johnny knew her. She was one of the prettiest gals around here and one of the nicest—I'm glad they got together and it worked out. Johnny was pretty lucky getting her—a lot of us have agreed on that, too. He certainly couldn't have done any better, and I'm certain she gave him a sense of stability. Where he grew up, their house was real small and his dad liked to bend his elbow a bit—hell, a lot—and then the Hammitts came along and helped him greatly. They loved him so much and they became like second parents to him, they didn't make it easy for Johnny, either. I remember going over to visit and he'd be weeding the garden or some other chore; I thought, *God, to get Johnny to do something like this they must really be special to him.*

My favorite baseball movie was *The Natural*, probably because it made me think of Johnny. The first part shows the young boy throwing baseball after baseball through a trap door in their barn. Johnny was a natural with all this ability but he worked hard at the fine points of the game. I'll always remember when the rest of us had taken our shower we'd find him still out there batting off a tee into the batting cage just to sharpen his stroke. He worked very hard to be the best that he could be—that's for sure. He had great natural talent, but his constant practicing made a big difference as well. He was always trying to improve his game. It wasn't that that made the difference, but I think that kind of attitude and determination is what made him so exceptional.

I was just Don Jones, the catcher. I'd have given anything to be Johnny Callison, the slugger, the major leaguer, to this day. When his name comes up now and then at functions I'm always amazed how everyone says, "Johnny and I played together—I played against Johnny Callison." I just sit back and smile inside, knowing that I really did and he was my friend. Like I said before, no one believes that either, because he was so good, and I can understand any such suspicions because I never could believe the things that he did on a field and I was there in the early years.

But as Johnny would say, "Wait a mintute, I wasn't all that great of a guy." One time I was driving my dad's Corvette and picked Johnny up. He wasn't used to that kind of a car. I let him drive and we went out to a place called The Bluffs. I'll never forget him putting his foot to the floor and jamming through those gears as he would a defensive line and the tears that started running out of my eyes from sheer fright. As we raced along Johnny kept yelling, "What's wrong Don?" in his drawl! "What's wrong!" He was always a gamer, and I was nearly shitting my pants on this occasion!

*　　*　　*

My teammates were really nice after the game. They shook my hand and everything. They really congratulated me, and Al Lopez told me, "You were right in there." His comment really made me feel good. But I got lucky because those balls were really just falling in there. In fact, Jim Piersall told me, "You're sure lucky. If I'd been playing right you wouldn't have got those hits. I didn't know anything about you—they told me you were a dead pull hitter." I took his comments pretty seriously, but then I found out what a character he was and realized Jimmy was giving me a "rookie" ribbing.

*　　*　　*

It was reported:

Charles Comisky, Jr., vice president of the Chicago White Sox, was quoted as saying from spring training camp in 1958 that Paul Richards of the Orioles had already tried to pry Callison from the White Sox. Comiskey said Richards's unsuccessful attempt was on January 19, 1958, when he and the Baltimore manager met with Commissioner Ford Frick after the Orioles hollered "damaged goods" and wanted to return pitcher Jack Harshman back for an outfielder named Calypso, or something like that, at Bakersfield last year. Comiskey said, "I told him that the name was Callison and not Calypso at Bakersfield. And I told him, " 'No way!' "

Chapter Two

Bakersfield's East High School to Indianapolis and Triple A Ball

Then out of the broken sun-rotted mountains of Arizona to the Colorado, with green reeds on its banks, and that's the end of Arizona There's California just over the river, and a pretty town to start it, Needles, on the river. But the river is a stranger in this place. Up from Needles and over a burned range, and there's the desert. And 66 goes on over the terrible desert, where the distance shimmers and the black center mountains hang unbearably in the distance. At last there's Barstow, and more desert until at last the mountains rise up again, the good mountains, and 66 winds through them. Then suddenly a pass, and below the beautiful valley, below orchards and vineyards and little houses, and in the distance a city. And, oh, my God, it's over . . . The people in flight from the terror behind— strange things happen to them, some bitterly cruel and some so beautiful that the faith is refired forever.. . . .

—John Steinbeck, *The Grapes of Wrath*

Once I was certain I'd receive a major league baseball contract, Dianne and I decided to get married. We had nearly three months of school left before our graduation, but circumstances were dictating that marriage would be the right avenue for us to pursue. We moved in with Dianne's grandmother, Henrietta (Etta) Petzolt, but I only knew her as "Nana."

She was the emotional support we needed, and we enjoyed our short stay there very much. When I received my sign-up bonus

Dianne and I began apartment hunting, and believe me, I was in no hurry. Nana took great care of me, making special meals all of the time—I really dreaded the thought of going without her homemade bread that she made every week. Furthermore, I didn't even know if Dianne could cook.

Graduation day came soon enough, and the baseball scouts from fourteen of the sixteen major league clubs came in right behind. Back in those days a representative from a professional ball club could not even talk to a prospect until he graduated from high school. I knew for a fact that I had been scouted for three years, but I just knew it by observation and what my coaches, teachers, and other people told me. So, now that I had my diploma in hand, they were quick to come knocking at my door, and their enthusiasm about me made it exciting for us all.

The day after graduation, baseball scouts were swarming around our place like bees from midmorning until midnight. They all operated basically the same way. For instance, the St. Louis Cardinal scouts kept telling me if I'd sign with them I'd be playing next to Stan Musial in a year or two. Wow! I loved to hear stuff like that—Stan the Man and me? Each set of scouts had their own special techniques and certain deals that made their offer special. I enjoyed listening to all of them. I was flattered not only by their comments about my ability and promises of a successful future, but also with their generosity in wining and dining Dianne and me. We were not accustomed to going out to fancy restaurants, and I didn't even know how to order, save proper etiquette. But I learned quickly, and I'll never forget how those scouts threw fifty-dollar bills around like they were yesterday's newspaper. All of it was overwhelming, and I would have liked to sign with each and every club because they were so nice to us. But I had good counsel, and never made any overtures or commitments to any of them.

Victor Manley, my history teacher, was a tall, stern gray-haired man with bushy eyebrows who had hailed from Illinois and was a Chicago White Sox fan. For some reason he had taken an interest in me, and it was at his urging that the White Sox first began to scout me. This was in my sophomore year. Sometimes in class, when he was giving out assignments, he'd slip by my desk to give me an article in the *Sporting News* about the White Sox. So I had the White Sox on my mind for three years already before the teams sent out their ambassadors. Manley kept his eyes on me, and when graduation was near he advised me that he had done his own research and determined that there were no great prospects in the White Sox farm system. At least not outfielders. He told me stars like Jim Rivera were on their way out and it would be a great opportunity to move into the Bigs quickly. I considered him a smart man, liked him because he was interested in me, and consequently was leaning toward the White Sox. I did challenge him, however, with the question: "What if another team offers me more money?"

In those days a major league club could only offer a ballplayer $7,000 to sign, unless they were going to put him right into the majors. Manley advised me that unless I got at least $25,000, I shouldn't consider any such offer because I would lose money in the long run. He explained to me how most of the young ballplayers who accepted a big bonus had a difficult transition from high school to the big leagues. These players found themselves sitting on the bench and securing little playing time. In baseball you must play to get better—most of these guys never made it because they never got to play. Additionally, Manley told me, the big clubs didn't like to pay out this big money because of the resentment of the veterans and the pressure it put on the young prospect. When he explained it all to me in the way that he did, it all made sense, and looking back, he was right as usual.

One scout in particular I'll never forget was Floyd Caves "Babe" Herman from the Philadelphia Phillies. I never even considered signing with the Phillies because they were a last-place team, and the thought of living in those big eastern cities didn't thrill me that much. But Babe Herman—wait a second. Here was a "real ballplayer" in his day. Babe had a lifetime batting average

29

of .324, and in two successive years he hit .381 and .393; however, his baserunning and fielding forged another legend. The records have it that Babe once doubled into a double play when the two runners who were on and Babe all slid into third base at the same time. On another occasion, a fly ball almost hit Herman in the head. Herman was revered by Dodger fans for his bumblings rather than his failings, but most of all because he was one of the best hitters in the game. I liked him, too, right off. On that June night, when scouts were all over our place, the Babe took a step up and offered to cook for everybody. What he was really doing, he told me years later, was spying on his competition. I was proud to talk to a really good ballplayer from the past and, had the Babe represented another team, it probably would have been difficult to refuse his offer.

Because my mind was pretty well made up, and with everyone offering basically the same amount of money, $7,000, I determined I would sign with the White Sox. Hollis Thurston, who stood somewhat stooped, with a kindly smile, and Doc Bennett, a military type who looked like President "Ike" Eisenhower, were the two that gave me the contract. But I was fortunate once again to have had Lorin Montgomery, Dianne's stepfather, to help me negotiate the deal a little bit further. Lorin had been a business man for years, and he took me aside to tell me that these guys had been following my baseball for three years. "They aren't going to give up now, so you need to ask them for a little kicker." The kicker was $3,000 cash under the table, and when they skinned that money off and laid it on the table, little did they know I would have signed anything they put in front of me. I was in tall cotton, it seemed, having a $7,000 check and $3,000 cash in hand. But my father-in-law helped me take it a step further. Bakersfield had a Class C team in town, and he advised me to request that I play ball right in my hometown that first summer. This made sense. Dianne was pregnant, which made it a bad time for us to relocate or for me to be away from home. I would be joining the team in midseason, so I figured the Sox wouldn't mind. They played in the California League (most of their opponents were located in the Valley) and I could start playing immediately. Thurston and Bennett did what they had to do to put the icing on the cake. As it turned out, the Bakersfield club was elated to get a heralded hometown boy on their team. It would certainly increase attendance because the owners of the teams in this league ran the organization to make money. Everything was set, including a guarantee by the Bakersfield ball club that I would have a fall and winter job after the season ended. The very next day I was in a Bakersfield Bears uniform and on my way.

*   *   *

Les Carpenter:

Johnny's the greatest player I've ever had. In his senior year he hit nine home runs, eleven doubles, two triples, and his batting average was .456. He was All-League, most outstanding player, the winner of the Sam Lynn trophy, and first recipient of the annual Jim Tyack award for best all-around athlete of Kern County.

Johnny was one of the most cooperative players I've ever had. He was a hustler, a team man, had a quick eye and a great throwing arm. But probably his greatest asset was his speed. He just seemed to have the ability to know where the ball was going to be hit. It was a sixth sense. He knew at the crack of the bat. He'd make lazy players out of the right or left fielders if they would let him. He got that much of a jump on the ball. Anything he tried, he learned very easily.

Our football coach, Migs Apsit, basketball coach, Jim Waterman, and I would get together once in a while to talk about Johnny. Migs called Johnny the most versatile and unpredictable player we'd ever had in football. Jim would say Johnny was one of the better ones we'd ever had in basketball, and we all concurred that he would have been an outstanding athlete in anything he tried, be it track, swimming, tennis, or golf. He was the kind of an athlete that was only satisfied with being the very best. He was the best baseball player I ever had and the best hitter I've ever seen.

*   *   *

Here I was in the minor leagues only a few days out of high school—18 years old and still playing ball with the guys older than me. It kind of reminded me of those Mexican games when I was just a young kid. But times were different now, and those old worries of what would become of my life because my environment seemed out of control had vanished—it was my turn to make it the best it could be. I was in control now, money in the bank and a bat on my shoulder. My wife, children, and I would have the best clothes, and my new 1958 Ford hardtop was sitting just outside the ballpark.

Bakersfield was in the California League and all of our opponents were just up the Valley—Modesto, Fresno, Salinas, Visalia, Stockton, San Jose—and our longest trip was to Reno, Nevada. When I started there were eighty-six games left in the schedule, and the manager immediately inserted me in the lineup in left field and batting third. I went on a tear right off, hitting safely in my first seventeen games even though there was a big difference in the pitching. I saw my first slider, and a slider is like a fastball that snaps out at the last minute. It fools you. In high school you're used to the big roundhouse curve. With a slider, the ball is right there and then it isn't. Sometimes a slider drops like Steve Carlton's. I've heard people say if no one had ever swung at Carlton's slider, he'd have walked everyone, but the ball is right there at that second—what are you going to do, look at it? Then, when you swing, the bottom falls out and you look "bush."

The minor leagues, then, had different levels of ball—it went from D ball, C ball, B ball, A ball, Double A and Triple A. So Bakersfield was just one jump above the lowest level, but it didn't matter that first summer, and I proved quickly I belonged at a higher level. But it was a good first experience, and I'm glad I saw both ends of the spectrum. It made me appreciate being in the major leagues even more.

We traveled in an old dilapidated bus driven by our trainer, a big fat Mexican fellow. About all he knew about medicine was handing you a Band-Aid if he thought you needed one. Also, all of the seats on the bus were broken. Some of the guys would sleep on the rafters that were originally there to stash luggage. On the road we stayed in crummy old run-down hotels. A typical type setup was two to a room which had one overhead light bulb, a toilet down the hall that serviced the whole team, and in places like Salinas there was only one bed to a room so we'd have to sleep with our roommate. Many times I thought, *I have to get out of here.*

I was home half of the time and, of course, I never felt like quitting because this was my dream—my way out—and I was determined to make it. The money was, at best, inadequate. We were paid once a month. I guess my pay was something like $400 per month, but that coupled with my bonus wasn't hay for doing what I liked to do best in the world—play baseball!

I remember looking around at most of the other players in Bakersfield and wondering how they made it. Most of them were twenty-six or twenty-seven years old and had been up and down in the minors. Many of them were married and they were located away from home or living in the shanties near Oildale. Dianne occasionally would go visit some of the players' wives, and she'd tell me how awful they were living. I understood, somewhat, why these players kept trying, though. Once baseball is in your blood it is a difficult thing to get it drained. I really don't think I'd have hung around in those conditions too long, but I'll never know, because fortunatcly it didn't work out that way for me.

As I said before, the California League was run by businessmen and they were in it for profit. Perhaps the older guys hung around just to keep the league going, and it was a proving ground for the big clubs to send their prospects. Vada Pinson played in the California League that year and hit .360. I hit .340, clubbed seventeen home runs, and had sixty-one RBIs. I was named the California League's outstanding rookie. It was a good start, but I always think about those older players who never went any further than that caliber of ball. Looking back, there would be guys that moved up and down in the minors. They were really good ballplayers, but whoever they were affiliated with just didn't need them. They would take these guys and move them to a certain minor league team just to take control over a hot prospect to get him on track. Once the hot prospect moved up they had no further need for the player that had put him on his way. There is no particular reason for the fairness or unfairness in the minor leagues as to what happens—it's just business and big business.

Feeling like millionaires, Dianne and I rented a beautiful apartment that was furnished with all new furniture for $70 a month, and we were very happy. Other than the times when I was on the road, being accommodated like a second-class citizen, we were living very well. I loved Dianne, our first baby was about to arrive, and I was off to a big start in my baseball career. I was learning more and more about the game, too. I'll never forget one of my first games which was played in Salinas.

I'm on second base and a ground ball is hit to third. I come running, hell bent for election, toward third base, and suddenly I see the third-bagger step on the base and throw the ball right at my head. I put on the brakes, duck, and think, *Oh shit, what did I do?* The third baseman came up to me after he completed the double play and said, "Keep your head down, Meat!" I'd been called a lot of things before but never "Meat," and I realized that I wasn't playing ball anymore for East High or in the Junior Baseball Association—professional ball was for all the cookies!

The season ended and I felt like I was on top of the world. Our daughter, Lori, was born in September, making our life complete, but then came reality around the corner one more time.

The Bakersfield club had promised me the sun and the moon. "We'll take care of you, Callison—don't worry 'bout nothing. We'll get you a good job during the off season." They got me a job alright. It was working for the county, putting cattle grates across the roads. One day I was pounding a spike into the road and it flew up and hit me in the eye. I was taken to the emergency ward, thinking my career had ended, and thought, *Yeah, they're really taking care of me*!

In retrospect, I guess I'd become somewhat spoiled with my recent successes. The Hammitts, the Carpenters, Dianne, Nana, Lorin, Babe (what I called Dianne's mother), and the blooming baseball career. That miserable job brought me back to earth, making me realize that I would have to work even harder. Thank God, Father Time turned a new year and brought baseball back into my life!

In January of 1958, I received a letter from Ray Johnston, general manager of the Indianapolis Indians, Triple A club of the White Sox. It was dated January 24, 1958, and enclosed was my contract for the 1958 season. There were also directions as to where to sign the contract and reminding me of the necessity of having one of my parents cosign since I was under the age of twenty-one. Additionally the letter explained that I was officially invited to the White Sox spring camp. I'd receive the details under separate cover. He wished me well for the coming season. My mother signed it with me and couldn't have been prouder. I was so thrilled to have shared that moment with her.

On February 9, 1958, by special invitation, we were invited to the Alexandria Hotel in Los Angeles where a committee composed of Los Angeles baseball writers named me for the annual Win Clark-Helms Athletic Foundation award. It was in honor of California's top first-year professional baseball player for 1957. The event was attended by famous players, both past and present, as well as many baseball dignitaries, including Hollis Thurston and Doc Bennett. I was proud and started feeling good about myself, again knowing I was on my way to the top.

*   *   *

35

Dianne Callison:

Johnny wasn't on the roster, he was just invited to training camp in the spring of 1958, so I wasn't allowed to go with him. It was a big step for his career, especially since he'd only played a few months in Class C ball in Bakersfield. Yet we had mixed emotions because we loved our apartment and things were quite cozy at home with the new baby, Johnny, and me. But our future was in the Midwest, so it seemed, and we prepared for Johnny to leave for Tampa, Florida, where the White Sox trained.

But there was another twist, and one that made me feel very proud. The White Sox were making a promotional movie and were featuring Johnny as this up-and-coming all-American kid. Just before he was to leave, cameramen were all over the place. I guess they wanted to project a scene from "rags to riches." The first scene of the movie was Johnny coming out of our apartment with an old suitcase and his mother following close behind. He embraced his mother, walked to the sidewalk, waved good-bye, as did his mother, and walked down the street. What seemed so funny is that Johnny just kept walking down the sidewalk as the camera followed him for about two blocks. Johnny kept looking back wondering how far they wanted him to walk? I couldn't be a part of this scene because in those days the mores were such that you shouldn't be married this early—plus, I guess, some of the effect would have been lost. It was like the young man going off to war, and who should be there but his mother.

On the day he left we stopped by the Hammitts and a few other places. They all wished us well and probably were as excited as we were that this was really happening. Johnny was only nineteen years old and going off to a big league training camp—it was a day to remember. I drove Johnny to Los Angeles, where, much to our surprise, we were met by Hollis Thurston and Doc Bennett at the airport. Their appearance made me feel more comfortable, and it certainly must have helped Johnny. He had never flown on an airplane and he was off to play ball with the likes of Nellie Fox,

Louis Aparicio, Jim Rivera, Billy Pierce, and Early Wynn. I felt that he was terrified, and he confided that in fact he was.

All of this hoopla with the movie cameras, etc., was putting more pressure on Johnny as well. Everywhere we turned there seemed to be a cameraman. So, I put Johnny on the airplane and I was left alone to wonder how he would make out. I wasn't too worried because he was going to play baseball, and he never had a problem being the best there was at this game. However, as I drove home my pulse raced, thinking about my husband in that airplane. I wondered was he that good at the game to be playing now with his childhood heroes? He was certainly the best ballplayer around these parts, but did he have the best competition? Only time would tell, during which I would be without my husband and my daughter's father. I could only find solace in the fact that baseball had been good to us recently, and if all worked well it would be our life and maybe an excellent one.

*   *   *

This was my first flight, and to be explicit, I was scared to death! It was a prop plane, a DC-3, I think. I even hated getting on that airplane. I can still remember the engines revving and the damn thing shaking like hell as we took off. I had a few fleeting moments when I thought about my father flying home on the shot-up B-17 he told us about—I should be as brave as him. But once we ascended I began feeling fairly comfortable. I found myself looking out the window and noticing all the ball diamonds that were laid out on the earth below. There were a lot of them, and I thought about all the kids that had played on each one of them. I was one in a million, perhaps, that was going cross country to a major league camp, and that fact was difficult to comprehend. It had all happened too quickly and suddenly; for just a moment, I wished I was a child again going to my first at bat. There was no pressure then. Just a getaway to do something I felt comfortable with. I was already beginning to feel the pressure of performing, and I didn't know, for the first time, if I could make it in baseball. I lit one cigarette after the other, and the flight seemed to take forever. The excitement of graduation, the scouts, signing a major league contract, success in C ball and baby Lori was fading as the old war-horse of a plane taxied up the runway in Tampa.

As I exited the plane in sunny Florida, I was holding my directions in hand. I picked up my luggage, hailed a taxi, and before I knew it I was at the hotel. I got my room and soon started meeting some of the other guys, wondering if they were as nervous as I.

The next day we boarded a chartered bus and it took us to the Al Lopez Ball Park. I had calmed down some, having met the other guys the night before, and realized they were no different than me. But those cameramen were still around, shooting scenes of me like I was the young Mickey Mantle, and I hated what they were doing. I just wanted to be one of the guys, not somebody special, that was supposed to perform extraordinarily. I was determined to live with it, though, and the other guys didn't give me that bad a time—in retrospect, I guess they wished they were me.

When I first walked in the ballpark there they were again, everything was planned. Al Lopez was there with Nellie Fox and Billy Pierce, and they welcomed me, specially, as the other guys just walked by probably wondering who the hell I was, Superman? I didn't know what to do as Fox, Lopez, and Pierce shook my hand and told me how great I was going to be—I just smiled sheepishly. Once this horseshit was over, and I'm sure the three of them thought of it this way as well, we got down to the business at hand. First on the agenda was batting practice—what a relief! But then when I got in the cage the damn cameras were there again. The first few pitches I just kept hitting off the top of the cage—I couldn't stand this pressure. Intuitively, however, some of the old-timers must have known what I was going through, and they just told me to relax. Then, I started to hit the ball like I always did and maybe even better.

After batting practice we were divided up in our groups: pitchers, catchers, infielders, and outfielders. We were instructed on various techniques. I started feeling more comfortable, even though those damn cameras were still on me, and started doing things more naturally. The instruction was good, but I was quick to find out that in the art of sliding and movement in the outfield I was way ahead of the others from the fine coaching I'd received from Les Carpenter. I was also quick to learn that I was as good and probably better than any of these prospects that were here—my confidence was building as a ballplayer.

In my first exhibition game, against the Cincinnati Reds, I got a hit my first time at bat. I couldn't believe that I was measuring up, and I realized at that moment I could really play major league baseball. I played in a lot of A games during those first few weeks and was respectable. Then, they sent most of the nonrostered players to Hollywood, Florida, on a bus to the minor league camp, and I was one of them. Remember, I had already signed with the Indianapolis Indians so it was their time, and again, perhaps I was relieved, being not ready for the Bigs for sure—more emotionally than physically! But I'd made a good show with the big club and I knew it—movies or not.

During the forties the New York Giants had several power hitters like Johnny Mize, Sid Gordon, and Walker Cooper. I thought about that when I dressed out in my Indianapolis uniform in Hollywood, Florida, knowing Walker Cooper, the guy that could scare the hell out of you the way he turned in his lips, would be our manager. Just like I watched Jim Landis hit a ball back through the box when Early Wynn was pitching batting practice, and Landis walked out of the box saying, "That's enough batting practice for me," Cooper put the fear of God in you.

Early Wynn was a big, mean Indian, and he'd been around a long time. He hated it when he was throwing a batting practice and someone hit the ball right at him. I saw him, one time, throw a ball right at a batter when he inadvertently hit the ball back through the pitching mound. Cooper was the pro and you just knew to respect that right off.

We arrived in Hollywood, Florida, via bus. We were taken to the hotel, where we were paired off and went to our rooms. Looking back, the White Sox didn't know the caliber of players they had. There was John Romano, Earl Battey, Norm Cash, Harmon Killebrew, myself, and several others that would all become future all-stars. And, two years later we'd all been traded for one of Bill Veeck's fanciful whims. We received further training, played more ballgames there, and then were flown to our respective minor league assignments to begin the 1958 season (all of the aforementioned to Indianapolis, Indiana).

In Triple A ball you had nearly as good treatment as if you were in the majors. Rather than traveling by buses and trains, you rode in airplanes. On that trip to Indianapolis I had time to think once again. I thought about the old pros, childhood heroes, who had seemed to go out of their way to help me. Nellie Fox had advised me to work on my defense. "It'll keep you in the game longer." Al Lopez, I just thought the world of him. The whole organization was simply class, and I looked forward to being a part of it forever. They called me "Rookie John," and all of them couldn't have been nicer to me.

There were a lot of old pros with the White Sox at the time; Larry Doby, Suitcase Simpson, Del Ennis, and Jim Rivera. They were all such real gentlemen. I'll never forget the time that Barry Latman, Suitcase Simpson, and I were taking a cab to the ballpark. When we arrived, Suitcase said he had the fare. Barry, for some reason, argued with him—it made no sense to me! Simpson decked Barry with one shot, and when we piled out of the cab the cabbie asked where the other guy was. "In the gutter," said Simpson. "When I say I got it, I got it."

My reminiscing ended as we landed in Indianapolis and we were whisked off to the Roosevelt Hotel. Again, we were paired off and assigned to a room, being told that we could stay until we found our own living accommodations. I seemed set, moving from Class C ball to Triple A, and now I could hardly wait to start playing and for Dianne and the baby to arrive to begin our new life.

*   *   *

Dianne Callison:

When I got the word from Johnny, my mother, Lori, and I headed across country from Bakersfield, California, to this unknown part of the world, Indianapolis, Indiana. We arrived on the outskirts of this city near one o'clock in the morning. Johnny had mailed me a map of Indianapolis, and we followed it into the city to the Roosevelt Hotel, where he was supposed to be staying. I parked the car in the driveway to the main entrance of the hotel and left my mother and the baby in the car. When I went to the front desk I asked, "Do the Indianapolis Indians stay here?" The night auditor said, "No!" I told him my husband was a member of the Indians, but it made no difference. He gave me an emphatic "No!" Being only eighteen years old myself I couldn't imagine anyone lying about such a thing. So I went back to the car and my mother and I discussed the possibility of Johnny giving us the wrong information.

Not knowing what to do, I started the car and we began to drive. Frustrated, I saw a bar and told my mother that someone in a bar must know where the Indianapolis Indians stayed. She cautioned me about going into a bar underage in a strange city, but I was determined and did it anyway. I was told that the Indians stayed in a hotel across the street from the Roosevelt. So we went there next, and when I approached their night auditor he told me that the opponents of the Indians stayed in his hotel. The real Indians stayed across the street at the Roosevelt. Thoroughly aggravated now, I went back to the car, told my mother of my findings, and we rode across the street to the Roosevelt again.

I was livid! And even at my young age I could be intimidating!

I told my story again with more vigor. "My husband plays for the Indians; his name is Johnny Callison. I have his eight-month old baby in the car, and the place across the street said the Indianapolis Indians stay here." Looking somewhat chagrined, he looked at his register and told me Johnny's room number was such and such. I dialed him on a house phone. Johnny answered and asked, "Where are you?"

Biting my lip, I answered, "I'm in the lobby of the hotel, but they won't let me see you!"

Johnny told me the room number and told me to get Babe (what he called my mother) and Lori and come on up. So, I went out, parked the car, and Mother, Lori, and I came into the hotel. We went to the elevator and were immediately halted by a security guard. "You can't go up there!"

I started explaining my situation again but it was to no avail. Irate, I went back to the desk! We got him on the phone again, and I told Johnny they wouldn't let me come up to see him and we were all in the lobby. He said, "I'll be right down."

Well, let me tell you, by the time Johnny got down to the lobby I was so angry that I was not even happy to see him.

He said, "I'll get a room for us and Babe."

I replied, "No way will I stay in this hotel!"

Knowing me as he did, he didn't argue. So, we all piled in the car and checked every place out down the road, and wouldn't you know it, there was not a vacancy anywhere. Three hours later, exhausted, and he with a game the next day, we slithered back into that hotel and got two rooms there. I would get an explanation later that a few years before, a ballplayer had been shot by a disenchanted lady fan, feeling she had been taken advantage of, and that was the reason for the intense security. Nevertheless, the experience had been awful, and at my age it was difficult to comprehend. But we survived, and Johnny's first year in Triple A ball was about to begin.

*　　*　　*

I didn't realize, at first, what a tremendous step it would be moving from Class C ball to Triple A. I probably had fooled myself, somewhat, because on the first day of spring training I hit five balls out of the park during batting practice. On the next day I hit two long balls, the first coming off Dixie Howell, and that ball was a high, arching shot which cleared the fence in dead center field, carrying at least 450 feet, so I was told. The second came off Dick Donovan, one of our aces, and that ball flew over the 377-foot marker in right center field. It was flat gone because none of the outfielders moved a step as they just turned around to watch it ride. I remember that ball seemed to draw everyone's attention. Pepper games stopped, players who were running in the outfield halted, and Al Lopez, our manager, disengaged himself from a conversation and moved behind the batting cage for a closer look. I remember leaving the batting cage that day with my hands blistered and bleeding. But that didn't matter, because I knew I was really hitting the ball, and there is no better feeling than when you meet the ball just right with your bat.

When it came time for the first game of the Grapefruit League, Al Smith, who had been acquired from Cleveland during the winter, had been penciled in as the lead-off hitter and starting left fielder. Al, however, had an ailment and was counted out for a week to ten days. Much to my surprise, Manager Lopez put me in the lineup for Smith, and here I was starting for the White Sox in the opening game. It didn't seem real!

I talked with Dianne on the telephone the night before the game to tell her the good news. I told her, kiddingly of course, Lopez was telling reporters that I hit like Ted Williams and Mickey Mantle. I didn't believe that, and I am sure Dianne didn't either, but it was fun to hear such kindly gossip. I also added that I was very lonesome. Dianne got quick word to our friends, family, and Les Carpenter. My former coach sent me a congratulatory telegram saying he would be sitting on pins and needles awaiting a report on the game. My first opponent was the Cincinnati Redlegs, and I went two for four my first game. Once again, I jumped off to a great start.

Even so, I had signed a contract with the Indianapolis Indians, and off to Hollywood, Florida, I went to continue my spring training with the Indians of the American Association. I met quite a bunch of guys there, too. Our outfielders were Ted Beard, Sam Mele, Joe Altobelli, and myself, of course. In the infield we had picked up Harmon Killebrew on option from the Washington Senators. We had John Romano and Earl Battey for catchers, adding even more long-ball power to those already previously mentioned.

I got off to a good start in Indianapolis. After the first 100 at bats I was hitting .247 but was leading the league in home runs with seven, and in RBIs with nineteen. Before the end of May I had hammered eleven homers, four doubles, three triples, and knocked in twenty-eight runs. There was a blurb in the *Chicago Sun-Times* about this time saying that between the five White Sox outfielders they had only seven homers and thirty RBIs. Once again, nice stories to hear, but Al Lopez and Walker Cooper, my manager at Indianapolis, said I wasn't quite ready for big league pitching. They were right. Before the end of June I went into a hell of a slump that almost sent me reeling back to Double A ball in Colorado Springs. During this spell we dropped nineteen of twenty-four games and dropped into the cellar of the American Association. Although, when I hit the ball, it generally went for a home run, I had managed only eight hits in my last thirty-four times up.

I had also had a rough time in early May when my average was down to a lowly .197. Ten days later, however, after a barnstorming of the Twin Cities, Minneapolis and St. Paul, I had raised my average 82 points to .279 when, in a five-game stint, I had batted eleven for twenty-two with three home runs. Saved by the bell! I started hitting again this time and was elected to start for the American Association all-star team in which I struck out three times.

I figured I could hit twenty home runs in any league, but it was my batting average that bothered me. I seemed to be always hovering between .250 and .275, and I thought I would hit for a better average. But I'd never seen such good pitching as they had in that league, and I worried—it was my nature.

My teammate, Ted Beard, told me to quit thinking about my average and home runs and just play ball. When I hit my twentieth home run—teammate John Romano had nineteen—we generated quite an interest for the fans as they thought we were competing with each other, and maybe we were. And as for Beard's remarks— I could never quit thinking about my average or home run total!

As the season drew near its end, all kinds of things were being said and written about me. I was being considered, along with others, for the "Rookie of the Year" in the American Association. Reporters kept comparing my size (five feet, ten inches and 170 pounds) to my power. They marveled at some of my tape-measure homers and said if I could learn to pull the ball I'd even hit more. My power alley was always straight away, and in most ballparks the deepest part of the field is usually in dead center. I hit only nine of my first twenty-five homers that year at Victory Field and that was because the center-field wall was 480 feet from home plate—I had several 400-plus outs that year. The other ballparks in the American Association had much shorter center-field fences and that is why I hit more home runs on the road. It seemed simple to me, but I always found myself explaining this mathematical concept over and over again to reporters, and they would always say, "Why don't you learn to pull the ball?" They also got on my base running, giving me credit for good speed (3.3 seconds from home to first), reporting that I had only stolen seven bases and would occasionally get trapped in a rundown. Oh well, I'd work on baserunning. They reported that my outfield range was wide, blessed with sure hands, and I had a strong arm. But I put too much arc on my throws from the outfield. I admitted that I had an awful lot to learn yet. And when the Rookie of the Year voting came in I was edged out by Willie Tasby, who had a better batting average, property of the Baltimore Orioles.

On September 5, 1958, after hitting my twenty-ninth home run of the season (and with that I won the home run championship in the American Association), I got the word I would be called up to the big club.

*   *   *

It was reported:

After Callison had hit safely in all of his first seven games since he'd joined the White Sox and was sporting a batting average of .360, Al Lopez was quoted as saying, "He looks as good at the plate as anybody else on our ball club right now and I'm not just going by the averages. . . . His youthfulness and lack of experience won't be any obstacle if he has big-league talent . . . there are fellows who have crashed the majors who were younger than Johnny and they made it big. . . . Mel Ott was only 16. . . . I like the way Callison swings at the plate. Some of the players say he looks a lot like Mickey Mantle in his batting style. . . . In the outfield he gets a wonderful jump on the ball. I'm convinced that he's going to be as good a ball hawk as Jim Landis. . . . "

Gene Mauch, who would become Callison's manager in the future at Philadelphia, was quoted at the end of the 1958 season as saying, "Of all the fine prospects I saw in the American Association . . . I rate John Callison of Bakersfield as a future star. . . . He has batting power like Mel Ott. He's a cinch. He hit .283 for Indianapolis in his first full year of organized ball. He hit twenty-nine home runs to lead the league and had ninety-three runs batted in. And to top it off he's only nineteen."

*   *   *

When the 1958 season ended I was tired from too much

baseball. I had done more than I thought I would when I left all alone on that plane in the spring for Tampa, Florida. It was exciting playing with the White Sox for those few weeks, but life in that hotel was pretty drab. Al Lopez approached me before I left, telling me he would like me to play winter league ball in Venezuela, but I told him I didn't want to go. He kept trying to push me by telling me I had a good chance of staying on the team if I kept improving, but I just wanted to go home as soon as possible. I never thought I'd say it, but I had had enough baseball for a while.

Dianne, Lori, and I drove home in our new 1958 Ford, and we stopped on the way to visit a few relatives and friends. But nothing looked as good as California when we finally arrived. We stayed with Dianne's mother at 2812 Alta Vista Drive, and, by the way, I quickly found out that she was my most loyal fan, outside of Dianne, of course. It was also good to get back among our former East High friends.

Looking back on my first real year of professional baseball, my greatest thrill and accomplishment, outside of my debut with the White Sox, was when I hit for the cycle at Minneapolis when they were thinking of sending me back to Double A in Colorado Springs. The toughest pitcher I faced was a guy from Wichita, a southpaw named Juan Pizarro. I struck out about every other time at bat against him, but I did manage to hit one home run off him. And then I'll always remember Jim Rivera when I first came up to the Sox. He was a seasoned major leaguer, and Lopez put me in his position right off. Rivera always tried to help me, and I must admit, he was one of the nicest guys I ever met.

Chapter Three

Winter Ball

He had feared that all of the untried men possessed a great and correct confidence. He now was in a measure reassured. . . . For days he made ceaseless calculations, but they were all wondrously unsatisfactory. He found that he could establish nothing. He finally concluded that the only way to prove himself was to go into the blaze. . . .

—Stephen Crane, *The Red Badge of Courage*

I was anxious to get the 1959 season going. I'd been working as a tile setter for the Turner Tile Company in Bakersfield during the off season, and that job was running a distant second to my baseball career. The White Sox had mailed me a contract for the minimum ($7,000) during the first part of January. I simply returned it, unsigned, with a note saying I thought I deserved a little bit more than the minimum. I would have never been a holdout, but I just wanted to see what they would do. I had played in eighteen games with the White Sox in 1958 and had hit .297. Even in my way of thinking, I thought I deserved more than I was paid the year before, especially since everyone was writing and talking about me. The writers were certain I'd make the Big Club right out of spring training this year. Sure enough, a week or two later, a new contract in the amount of $8,500 arrived. I was elated, signed it, and Dianne and I began to make plans to leave for Tampa,

Florida, on February 14, 1959—Valentine's Day!

*   *   *

Dianne Callison:

Johnny was officially a rookie in 1959. He was listed on the roster this year so I could go to Florida with him as a player's wife. It was an exciting time, as the experts were already picking Johnny to be the American League rookie of the year. Casey Stengel had been quoted that Johnny was a cinch to start in left field for the White Sox this season, and what better authority could there be than Casey? We'd been reading articles in various papers and the *Sporting News* that manager Al Lopez was looking for the youth to bring the Sox the '59 flag. He named Johnny, Barry Latman, and John Romano as those youngsters that he would be counting on, and Johnny was named first. We couldn't have been up any more than we were when we headed out for Tampa that spring of 1959.

During camp we stayed at the Venesian Palm Hotel near the Tampa airport. It was very nice and we had good company in the Jim Riveras and Ron Jacksons. Johnny had an excellent camp, and time passed quickly as the baby and I enjoyed the delightful Florida sun. Johnny was featured in the *Baseball Digest*, in the March 1959 issue, and sure enough, he was notified that he'd made the Big Club and we'd be heading for Chicago. Before he flew up to Chicago with the team he'd given me two maps, one for getting from Tampa to Chicago and the other a map of Chicago directing me to the Piccadilly Hotel on the South Side.

It was pretty frightening to think about driving across the country alone with the baby, but I had no problem traveling from Tampa to the outskirts of Chicago, and when I began making my descent into Chicago's Loop it was around midnight. It seemed I just drove and drove and the city seemed so vast and scary. Finally, I found myself on this wide boulevard near a lake, and since it was well lighted, I just stopped the car to try get my bearings straight. I was not parked there long when, thank God, a police car pulled up behind me. He put on his flashing lights and eased up to my side of the car. I told him I was lost and that I'd just driven up from Florida and was trying to find the Piccadilly Hotel on the South Side where I was to meet my husband, Johnny Callison (who played for the White Sox). Meanwhile, he was examining my California driver's license. He then walked to the rear of the car to check out my license plates. When he returned, he shined a flashlight into the backseat of the car and saw the baby lying there in her seat. "Oh," he said, "you have a baby. Well, lady, you can't park here—no one parks on Lake Shore Drive. I think you better follow me. I'll take you to the Piccadilly Hotel."

This was one time I wished I would have asked for someone's name because this kindly man took me to the hotel, got a doorman to unpack my car, and stayed there with me the whole time until I was safely settled. I was so scared until he arrived that night, and when I think about the story I told the guy—having come from Florida, California tags, California license, and I was the wife of one of the White Sox ballplayers—well, it must have sounded a likely story.

When I woke up the next morning I was even more terrified. The South Side of Chicago is not the finest part of town, and I wondered if I would ever dare go out of our room when Johnny wasn't home. I knew I wasn't going to like it there and was going to insist on Johnny finding us better accommodations really soon. But that is where we stayed, and the season got off to a start with Johnny having a difficult time with consistency. I think he was trying too hard, and when they went on a road trip to Cleveland sometime in May I received a call from Johnny saying he was sick as a dog.

He told me he had the Asian flu and the White Sox had sent a doctor out to the hotel to examine him because he couldn't even get out of bed. For some reason Johnny had a difficult time shaking that flu bug, and he just couldn't get his strength back. By the first part of June he was only hitting .190. We were informed, because of his condition, that we'd be going back to Indianapolis until he could get his strength back. Funny, this was almost welcome news to me as I wanted to get out of that hotel in Chicago more than anything else at that point.

It turned out to be one of our most pleasant baseball summers. When we arrived in Indianapolis one of the guys on the team, Carl Thomas, told Johnny he was being sent to a team in Arizona. We moved into his apartment, which was the entire second floor of a huge house on a pig farm right behind the "Indy 500" speedway. It was a large brick home out in the middle of farmland where the owners raised pigs and corn. It probably doesn't sound that great, but compared to a hotel room in Chicago's South Side where I was afraid to walk out of my room, it was a big improvement. We did enjoy it there, and the only thing that scared me was an owl that "whooed" in the tree outside our bedroom window when Johnny was on the road.

*   *   *

My stroke returned in Indianapolis and I was hitting .299 when they brought me back to the Big Club in August. This was just past the deadline, of course, where if the Sox won the pennant I couldn't be rostered for the World Series. I contributed significantly during the month of September. During the stretch run I had some clutch hits. Sure enough, we won the pennant and my contribution was so appreciated that the team voted me a small share of the World Series money. However, when management advised me that if I wanted World Series tickets I'd have to pay for them, I just didn't feel any part of the team anymore. I told Dianne, "Shit on it. Let's go home! I don't even want to see the Series." She protested some, but not enough, and we packed up our belongings to head west.

We traveled with nearly everything we owned except the extra sheets, towels, and clothes which we shipped in steamer trunks. So, when we left Chicago our car was packed to the hilt, leaving just enough room for the baby to be comfortable in the backseat and Dianne and I up front. For some reason we took a northerly route for the coast, and I had driven for some ten to twelve hours straight when Dianne took the wheel. It was early morning and we had just passed through South Dakota entering Wyoming when I fell asleep.

About six o'clock in the morning we were nearing Cheyenne, Wyoming, when a light snow began to fall. Dianne had woken me up a few minutes earlier to look at the snow. It was the first time she'd ever seen snow and she thought it was so pretty, but I was exhausted so I dozed off again. Shortly thereafter, Dianne pulled out in the left lane to pass a diesel truck and she was probably going only twenty miles an hour. Suddenly, I was awakened by her screams—she had accelerated the car and the back wheels began to fishtail, causing the car to begin sliding across the other three lanes of the road. I started yelling, "Don't hit the brakes! Don't hit the brakes!" But then, when we came to the side of the road, there was a huge ditch and she intuitively slammed the brakes. The car spun around and we begin sliding across the road in the other direction to an embankment, where we tumbled end over end into a gulley. The car landed on its roof and we were upside down, conscious and seemingly uninjured.

The guy driving the tractor-trailer stopped to help us. At first he couldn't get the car door open, but then he gave it a fierce yank while I kicked it on the other side, and the door fell open. We climbed out, but the baby was still in the backseat seemingly alright. She had four or five blankets wrapped around her and was lying on a mattress. When the car turned upside down everything had come down on top of her, so she was pretty secure because it was mostly clothes. I finally reached through the back window and fished her out of our demolished car. The baby was fine, other than a slight bump on her head. But Dianne was walking around out in the snow without her shoes when the Wyoming Highway Patrol arrived.

The Highway Patrol officer put us in his car and took us into Cheyenne to a Chevrolet dealer. He arranged to get the car towed. Since Lori had a little bump on her head, he then took us to a doctor to get her examined. Afterwards he took us to breakfast and back to the Chevrolet dealer because most of our belongings were in the car. Aware of the fact the car was practically totaled, we gathered what we needed, put it in the patrol car, and the officer took us to a motel. After we checked in he took us back to the Chevrolet dealer, where we gave away the stroller, crib, and other things cumbersome to ship. He took us to an Army/Navy store where we bought a trunk to ship what we couldn't carry on the plane to California. When the kindly officer dropped us back at the motel I remember just being relieved that we were safe once again.

Every time I hit a home run in Indianapolis there was this guy who gave me a silver dollar piece. I must have had forty or so silver pieces in the car and they were the only things missing when we retrieved our belongings from the car. The next day we boarded an airplane and flew home, leaving our new car, the baby things, and my silver pieces behind. When we arrived in California we had no car, and, as it turned out, we didn't really need one. I had made arrangements with Louis Aparicio to play winter ball for his dad's team in Maracaibo, Venezuela. We were required to report in just a few weeks and since we were carried under my father-in-law's insurance policy, I left my car problems with him.

The White Sox lost the World Series to the Dodgers, and we were on our way to Venezuela. We boarded a dilapidated old prop plane in Los Angeles for an eighteen-hour milk run. Up and down—land and take off. During stopovers we'd look out the window to see armed guards lining the runways. I mean, they were soldiers with rifles. I kept thinking, *My God, what have I gotten us into*? When we finally reached our destination we were met by Les Moss, a reserve catcher for the Sox, and he took us to the Americana Hotel, where we stayed for two days. I just kept thinking about those days a year or two earlier when the Sox's higher-ups kept telling me, "Don't worry about nothing, Johnny, we'll take care of you." Yeah, they were really taking care of me, alright!

*   *   *

Dianne Callison:

On the third day Les Moss came by to pick up Johnny to take him to the ballpark. He had secured an apartment for us and told me, "Dianne, now all you have to do is take a cab to the very bottom of this hill and you'll see the apartment building. It's called the—I don't know what it's called!" Well, I took a cab and Lori and I got in it, saying, "Please take us to the apartments at the bottom of the hill." This seedy-looking cabbie started driving, and the next thing I know we were circling a big lake and I started screaming, "I want to go to the apartments at the bottom of the hill!" He turned around and started shouting at me in Spanish. I was scared to death, but I started screaming back at him while he turned the car around and took us to the apartment. We'd been in the car for forty-five minutes and I was livid. When we finally pulled up to this rinky-dink apartment building I found Johnny and Les standing on the lawn laughing and drinking a beer. I got out of the car with Lori, mad as hell, leaving the Mexican cab driver screaming for his money in Spanish. Les Moss, who could speak fluent Spanish, went over to the cab and sent the guy angrily on his way because he had paid him very little.

While I was trying to calm down, Les did the worst thing he could have done. He suggested that we go in to look at our apartment. When we first walked into the place I was stunned. At first glance the place was simply filthy. There were two rooms with two double beds, one chest, a wooden-framed sofa with a ripped cushion, and one chair. In the kitchen there was a table with chairs. There were a couple of holes cut into the walls that served as windows, with bars, like a jail cell, to protect us from the environment—no windowpanes, just those bars in the open air.

Determined to make the best of this pigpen, I started to clean the stove. I had Johnny pull it out from the wall, and when he did, a million roaches scurried around the floor—big roaches. While I shivered, Johnny ran down to the manager's office to get some bug spray. Mr. Clean was the big insect and rodent product down there. In fact, people would drive around our area all the time in old run-down cars displaying a placard of Mr. Clean scribbled on a piece of cardboard atop their roof. Jack, the apartment manager, soon came up to our apartment with all kinds of Mr. Clean and a garden hose. "Hose the place down first," he said. Jack hooked up the hose to a spigot on the laundry tub and started hosing the whole apartment down. It was just something that was difficult to believe. The floors were cement, though, so nothing could be ruined. Once everything was hosed down, Johnny and I took scrub brushes to the floors, walls, and everything else in that dreadful dwelling. We worked for two days cleaning, and then we bombed the place with various bug sprays. When we were finished the place was clean, but the odor of bug spray was so overpowering it was difficult to breathe.

Feeling good that the place was finally rid of insects, we looked forward to a more comfortable evening of rest. We had been warned to bring enough clothes, etc., with us because the prices for such goods would be very high, so, consequently, I had purchased a new pair of slippers before we left California. I left them on the floor beside the bed when we retired that evening, and when I woke up the next morning I put my feet into the slippers. My toes popped right through the end of them. I couldn't quite figure it out for a moment, and then when I showed Johnny he said, "Rats!"

Another shiver went up my spine as I jumped back into the bed while Johnny stalked the room looking for the critters. But there were none to be found, of course, so he said, "Let's have breakfast."

I was still frozen stiff as I held the baby close to me. Then, I heard Johnny yell, "Shit!" When he opened the oven door to get a pan, a big rat was staring him right in the face. That did it—we ran across the hall to Les Peden's apartment to tell them of our woes. They advised us they had just gotten rid of their rats. Les pulled out some huge rat traps and a can of rat poison, and he and Johnny went across to our apartment for a rat kill. They put poison under the dresser in the bedroom and under the stove in the kitchen. They set traps in the secluded corners of the apartment and in back of the stove. The next morning Johnny checked out the poison and the trap by the stove. The rats had eaten the poison, licked up every bit of it, and then ate the three apples that were sitting on the kitchen table. No sign of rats, however!

As luck would have it, Johnny left on a road trip the next day, and road trips there were practically tours of South America. These were not pleasure trips, either. One was a nine-hour ride in a crowded taxi through jungles and mountains to a town at the Colombian border. We had put the two double beds together after the rat scare because we were afraid for Lori. When I thought the baby was sleeping safe and sound the first night Johnny was gone, I went to the Pedens' to play cards. Peden's team hadn't made the trip to Colombia, so Les had set traps all over the place for me during the day. I left our apartment door open so I could hear Lori, and suddenly, while we were playing cards, I heard a scratching sound coming from our place. We stopped playing for a few seconds, listened, and heard the scratching sound again. I got up and ran across the hall to be met by this huge rat; it must have been a foot long and was dragging this bulky trap across the room. I yelled for Les, and he came running in and grabbed the trap, which caused the rat to drop right on the floor in front of me. Then, I watched Les smash the thing to death with his foot right before my eyes. I was shaking again as Les calmly said, "These damn things must be getting in here from somewhere." He checked around to find big holes by the drains on the back porch. He stuffed some newspapers around the drains and set some books around the area. We never had rats after that, nor did we have bug problems. However, when the wind blew hard we had leaves and dirt all over our apartment. We had no hot water, and big lizards would lie on the branches of the trees outside our windows to look directly at us— eyeball to eyeball.

*   *   *

Venezuelans think Americans are assholes. All we wanted for Christmas was a turkey dinner and a tree. We had both, and when we were partying, they would come by looking at us, thinking, *Those gringo assholes*. Their Christmas is like our Fourth of July. The Venezuelans were shooting firecrackers, running around screaming, and looking at us like we were crazy. Eventually, we got sick of them looking at us, so we got some Roman candles and started shooting at them. They didn't know we were trying to hit them, and I guess it was good that they didn't.

Maracaibo was an awful place to live and play ball. The pay was good and the experience was necessary, but I would have never done it again. The name of our club was the Rapinas, which sounded pretty neat to me at first. A rapina is a bird, and I always liked birds. I soon found out, however, that this particular bird was what we North Americans call a buzzard. This was kind of disappointing, but I had found my way to Maracaibo through Louis Aparicio.

He was the greatest player I ever saw play the position of shortstop and was a pretty good hitter as well. Louis made the Hall of Fame not too long ago and made the shortest and probably the best speech ever: "Thank you!"

Well, Louis's family, the Aparicios, owned our ball club. They were crazy people and took this baseball pretty seriously. I was standing out in right field one night and heard all this commotion to my left. It was people seated below, throwing their chairs up at people above them, and the people above were dropping their chairs on the people below. When I returned to the dugout after the

57

inning I said to the center fielder, "Did you see that shit out there in right field?"

He grinned, saying, "Those are the Aparicios—they all hate each other!"

I was hitting around .300 down there and playing good ball. We went on another road trip sometime in January, pushing hard to make the play-offs. The day before I came home, Les Moss's wife knocked on our apartment door and told Dianne that I had been traded to the Philadelphia Phillies. When I walked in that night, tired and cranky, Dianne said, "Guess what?"

I said, "What?"

Dianne said, "You've been traded."

I refused to believe her even though she handed me the newspaper Les's wife had given her. It was written in Spanish, so I couldn't read the damn thing. But when I saw my picture and Gene Freese's with the headline reading boldly, CALLISON POR FREESE, I knew I was in trouble. I went right to bed.

The next morning I got up and went down to the manager's office to ask him to translate the story. When he did I was very disappointed. It was the worst feeling I've ever had in my entire baseball life. The White Sox had abandoned their grand plans for me. I was confused and just couldn't understand.

Why? I knew only that I had chosen to sign with the White Sox because they had seemed to my history teacher, Victor Manley, and me to be a great organization. They had a great need for young outfielders because their club was aging. What did I do wrong? I felt that being traded was one and the same as being cast off. I became depressed. It was my first failure in athletics, so I felt. After three years of professional baseball I had traveled a good part of the world. Now I felt not too far removed from the hot streets of East Bakersfield.

To make matters worse, a few days after I learned I'd been traded, I charged in for a sinking liner and dove for the ball—and I never dove for a ball. My knee wrenched right under me in the sandy Venezuelan soil. I fell forward on my face, feeling an ex-cruciating pain welling up in my knee. I limped into the clubhouse, where the team's witch doctor was sitting drinking a beer. He took some red solution out of a bottle and rubbed it on my knee like a complete jerk. He actually was a proclaimed witch doctor and had come right out of the jungle like several of the guys who played on the team. Some of these guys used to shit right between the toilets—they didn't even know why the toilets were there. We never showered in the clubhouse—it was simply too filthy. We came to the park in our uniforms and we went home in our uniforms.

The next day I asked Louis Aparicio to take me to a real doc-tor, as I could hardly walk. We went to the doctor, and this quack told me I needed my knee drained. He screwed a harpoon into the knee area to drain the fluid, and suddenly I felt this instrument touching my kneecap—I got the chills. So, he pulled it out and I let him screw it in again. The same thing happened. I got faint and passed out. When I revived, this double-asshole tells me I'm aller-gic to novocaine. I told him I'd been taking novocaine for years. "You screwed up, you jerk, and I'm getting the hell out of here!"

The team begged me to play but I couldn't. The team had made the play-offs, and I did want to play but I just couldn't. In retrospect, I don't know what I was feeling. I was so down and out about being traded. I think I was more emotionally stung than physically. But the combination thereof gave us little alternative. Plus Dianne had had it! At my wife's urging (and she was right), I told them I was leaving. Then we couldn't get our passports. It was frightening! Finally, I went to Aparicio. I told him that I'd been traded and I needed to get home to a qualified doctor or my career could be over. I don't know what Louis did, probably talked to his crazy family, but we had the passports shortly thereafter and we were on our way.

We boarded that same old ragtag plane to return and were told that it would be at least a twenty-one-hour flight. The thought of twenty-one hours on that plane seemed unbearable, but more desirable than staying in Maracaibo. We didn't get very far before it was announced that the air pressure in the cabin was fading and we would be flying really low, landing in Panama City. I'll never forget how I thought my ears were going to explode. We had purchased a couple of parrots in Maracaibo and had put them in a basket, taking them on the plane with us. When we landed in Panama City they wouldn't let us take the parrots to the hotel with us. We had to leave them at the airport, and when we arrived the next day, there was cardboard all around the basket. During the night the parrots had gotten loose and security people had run them down to save them for us.

I don't know why I liked those parrots so much. All they did was whistle, say hello, and squawk. I liked them so much, though, that when we finally arrived in Los Angeles and the airlines said we couldn't fly to Bakersfield with birds on the plane, Babe (Dianne's mother) drove down to pick us up. Maybe I felt I had to salvage something from our recent life in the jungle.

Once again it was good to be home in Bakersfield. Reality would soon set in once again very quickly, though. No car! No White Sox! Philadelphia? It was my last choice! In three years I went from my first choice to my last choice and I felt very let down.

My father-in-law had been through some grief with my car. One insurance man had gone to Wyoming to evaluate the damage, but he quit the company and nothing more was done about the situation. We called the dealer in Wyoming, and they said the car was ready but we had to be in Florida in a week. As an alternative, we went to a Pontiac dealer in Bakersfield. We purchased a new car, using the old one as a trade, knowing the moment we did, we were getting ripped off. But it had been that kind of a year, and when I thought things couldn't be any worse, I realized that it was time to try our fortune in Philadelphia.

En route to Florida I kept thinking about my first trip there— the White Sox—the movie in which I was promised $200 to perform. Well, I got a copy of the movie—being the young Mickey Mantle. I thought about Norm Cash, John Romano, Don Mincher, and Earl Battey. They had all been traded from the Sox, too. The guy I had trusted the most, Charley Comiskey, Jr., had been sold out by his sister to baseball man Bill Veeck. Veeck's position was to bring in some veterans to try win the pennant and maybe the series—this year! What a fool! Poor Charley!

I found solace in the fact that Charley would never have traded me, but his damn sister had 51 percent of the club and I wondered why.

Earl Battey! I thought about Earl again. He had the greatest arm I'd ever seen. When we'd won the pennant in 1959 he made me a bet. "Johnny," he said. "I'll bet you my puny share of the Series against your puny share. I will stand flat-footed at home plate and throw the ball over the center-field fence."

I thought about his proposal for a second or two and declined: "No, I don't think so."

Earl laughed and threw the ball easily over the fence!

I knew I was going to miss those guys. My knee was still hurting me, and I was wondering if I could still make it!

Chapter Four

Those "Fightin' Phillies" at 21st and Lehigh

There is no steady unretracing progress in this life; we do not advance through fixed graduations, and at the last one pause: through infancy's unconscious spell, boyhood's thoughtless faith, adolescence's doubt (the common doom), then skepticism, then disbelief, resting at last in manhood's pondering repose of IF. But once gone through, we trace the round again; and are infants, boys, and men, and IFs eternally. Where lies the final harbor, whence we unmoor no more?

—Herman Melville, *Moby Dick*

We arrived in Clearwater, Florida, only to realize that there was no place for us to stay. There was not one motel in the area that had a vacancy. We stopped at one place only to be rudely encountered by an elderly lady who said, "If we did have a vacancy you couldn't afford it." Her smart remark was enough to make me pull off into a rest spot, where Dianne, Lori, and I slept the night in the car. I remember thinking I was a big league ballplayer, but I hadn't quite pictured it this way. I was very bitter about being traded and I didn't want to play for the Philadelphia Phillies. My knee was still killing me, and my mind began to settle with the idea that this just wasn't going to work out for me. It was February 1960, less than three years off the streets of

East Bakersfield, and I felt like my career was already over.

The Robert Carpenter family owned the Phillies at the time, and the "old man" had just hired John Quinn from the Milwaukee Braves to be the new general manager. Quinn had put one of the finest teams in baseball history together in Milwaukee, bringing them the world championship in 1957. He had done it by developing a fine farm system and making shrewd trades. I was his first big deal, and I wished he'd have left me the hell alone. I knew nothing about Philadelphia other than the fact they were the worst team in baseball, and I had just come from the best in the American League. I'd never really been on winners before—we had won our share in high school, but I didn't learn how to win with the Bakersfield Bears or at Indianapolis. I guess I got spoiled right off when I went to the Bigs. I began thinking that getting postseason checks was the way it was supposed to be when you had really made it. I understood from the get-go there would be no postseason checks at Philadelphia. Perhaps I was more frightened about not knowing anyone—it was like starting over. Dianne and I found an apartment over someone's garage in Clearwater, and I reported to spring training. I'll always remember meeting John Buzhardt, a pitcher who had just been traded to the Phillies. On that first day we just stood there together, looking around trying to spot someone we might know. We shook our heads, and I said to him at least he'd be playing in the same league.

Looking back, there were a lot of great guys in my first Phillies year. Catchers were Jimmie Coker, Clay Dalrymple, Cal Neeman; first base were Pancho Herrera, Ed Bouchee, Dave Philley, Harry Anderson; second base were Tony Taylor and Bobby Malkmus; shortstop were Ruban Amaro, Joe Koppe, Bobby Wine; third base were Al Dark, Ted Lepcio, Lee Walls; outfielders were Ken Walters, Bobby Del Greco, Bobby Gene Smith, Tony Curry, Tony Gonzalez, Wally Post, Joe Morgan, and this new guy Johnny Callison; pitchers were Robin Roberts, Dick Farrell, Gene Conley, Art Mahaffey, Chris Short, John Buzhardt, Curt Simmons, Dallas

Green, Jim Owens, Don Cardwell, Jack Meyer, and others. We would finish in last place with a record of 59–95, and the Pittsburgh Pirates would win the pennant with the reverse record. The Pirates would also win the World Series with Bill Mazeroski's dramatic home run in the seventh game over the Yankees.

Some of the above-mentioned players weren't there at first during spring training. Quinn was doing a lot of trading, some good and some bad. The worst was sending Curt Simmons to St. Louis. But these were the guys I played with my first year in Philadelphia, and there were some up-and-coming players, as time would soon enough prove. Eddie Sawyer, our manager through spring training and the first regular season game, didn't think so. After our opener he said, "I'm forty-nine and I want to see fifty." He quit! Andy Cohen took over for one game and then Quinn brought in a thirty-four-year-old manager named Gene Mauch.

Every team has a character. Ours, in 1960, was Bobby Del Greco. Bobby was a good outfielder but a lifetime .229 hitter. He was up and down from the minor leagues, having a difficult baseball life. But he was a great, good-natured clubhouse needler. When training first started, he picked right up on my difficulty making long-distance throws from the outfield. What he didn't know, of course, was that my leg was injured. He was quick to nickname me "Candy" as he said my throws from the outfield looked like lollipops. Naturally, a clubhouse writer picked up the name and it got around. Unfortunately it connoted not only a weak arm, but gave the impression that I had been spoiled rotten by the Sox publicity.

I closed my mind to this horseshit, though it bothered me, and began hitting the cover off the ball in the exhibition games, thanks to a former Pirate player named Paul Waner. Waner was just a little skinny guy when I met him, and I couldn't imagine what he could teach me about hitting. I would soon find out that in his playing days he was known as "Big Poison," and in nearly 9,500 career at bats he had a lifetime batting average of .333. He was a left-handed hitter who was known for his hard living and an uncanny ability to spray hits in any direction he chose. The Phillies had hired him this spring to be the batting instructor, and he was the most influential hitting teacher I ever had!

He had a way of putting it so simply. He walked up to me one day when I was lunging at pitches and told me I was swinging too hard. Waner had seven words that summed up all that he tried to teach me: "Down on the ball, belly button around." What he was saying was that I ought to come down on the ball and that my hips should swing in such a way that my belly button would face the pitching mound at the moment the bat contacted the ball. Once I got my belly button around I was out in front of the ball, my bat was level, and everything was taken care of. In future years, when I was at the top of my game, I always gave Paul Waner the credit for my successful hitting. Funny, Waner hailed from a place called Harrah, Oklahoma. Maybe that's why he liked me. We Okies got to stick together! He shared with me every trick of the hitting trade during that spring training. He told me, for example, that in his day, batting left-handed, he often pulled the first pitch foul, slashing it into the first-base stands as hard as he could. The pitcher then would deduce that Waner was hoping to pull the ball down the line, then would come back with an outside pitch. The foul ball had been Waner's way of making certain he knew what the next pitch would be. When he wanted an inside pitch he'd foul off the first pitch to the opposite field. All this was new to me and I liked to listen to Paul Waner talk baseball. This was a particular treat for me in another way as well. When I went into my slumps in Indianapolis I'd go to Walker Cooper, our manager, who had been a pretty good hitter himself in his day, to ask for advice. He'd just say, "It comes from the top. I can't touch you kid—no one can touch you—we're told not to mess with your swing." I hated that! I wondered what I was supposed to do—I was only nineteen years old then!

I juiced seven home runs during spring training, and even though the club knew my knee was hurting and that I probably couldn't play that much at first, I made the club and we were on our way to Philadelphia. Little did I know that it was going to be 1959 all over again! The season had no more begun when we were playing a game against the Cincinnati Redlegs at Connie Mack. I was on second base when one of my teammates hit a grounder up the middle. I hesitated when I rounded third base, but Gene Mauch waved me home. The on-deck batter did not signal me either to slide or score standing up. I went in half up and half down. I crashed into Ed Bailey, the Redleg catcher, six foot two and two hundred five pounds of solid muscle, tearing the tendons in the same knee I'd injured in Venezuela. I was immediately taken to Temple University Hospital and put in traction.

*   *   *

Dianne Callison:

When we first arrived in Philadelphia, Johnny, Lori, and I stayed at the Walnut Plaza Apartments. Soon thereafter Johnny received a list of places available to live and we began house hunting. We found this two-story Colonial-type home in Havertown and rented it. It was a new, big city, and I didn't know my way around at all, so I wasn't going to the games when the season first started. Lori was a handful now, too, and it just seemed better to listen to the games on the radio. On this particular day I was tending to Lori and listening to the game and I heard, of course, that Johnny had been hurt and taken out of the game. After the play I was doing something with Lori and didn't hear the report that Johnny had been taken to the hospital. Some very nice neighbors, Joe and Gloria Skurla, came to the door to tell me that they had heard Johnny was in the Temple University Hospital. I was shocked, of course, and thought it was strange that I hadn't been called. But we had just had our telephone hooked up, and I found out later that Johnny didn't know the telephone number or our address.

Joe and Gloria offered to stay with Lori and gave me directions to the hospital. I was scared to death to drive through north Philadelphia where I'd never driven alone before to make my way to the hospital. But I did it and found Johnny lying in traction when I arrived.

The doctors told me Johnny would be alright but would be out of action for some time. When I left for home another great fear came over me. I realized I would have to stay alone in the house that night with Lori. I'll never forget that first night alone. I thought I heard noises in the basement and sat up all night with a baseball bat propped up in bed. I was only twenty-one, alone in a strange big city, and there was nobody. We didn't know a soul. Fortunately, I received a telephone call from Kathy Del Greco, whose husband had tagged Johnny with the "candy" label. She asked, "Are you doing alright?" Fighting back the tears I said yes, but I cried myself to sleep every night.

Kathy said, "Look, I went through that before; I know how it feels. Bring your little girl and come over and stay with us." I protested, of course, because Kathy was pregnant with her sixth child, but Kathy would not take no for an answer, and I really didn't want her to. It would be the beginning of a great friendship and pattern. During the time Johnny was in the hospital, and when he was on the road that year, I would go to the Del Greco's at dusk and return home at dawn.

*   *   *

Bobby Del Greco:

I thought Johnny was a real good ballplayer when I first saw him during spring training in 1960. I watched him as everyone else did, because we'd heard all this stuff about him from Chicago and we'd given up a hell of a ballplayer in Gene Freese to get him. But I could see right off he was a good hitter, had a real good arm, and ran well, too. I knew right then he was going to be a real good ballplayer. He worked hard at it, too.

67

He'd get to the ballpark early for extra hitting practice.

I tagged Johnny with a few names that stuck for a while, and he was so young I don't know if it bothered him or not. I did that to everybody, though. We became real good friends and we were roommates for a while during that 1960 season. I played alongside of him for a while. I played center field and he was in left. I could tell he was a real competitor the way he'd go after balls. Like I said, he had a good arm and ran real well. I knew his hitting would come around as soon as he was playing regularly. Funny I should say his hitting would come around—he batted better than .250, and most of us would've been pleased to accomplish where he was disappointed. Hell, he worked so hard and I thought he made himself a better ballplayer than he really was because he worked at it so hard.

Johnny was a pretty quiet kid and kept to himself. Some of us older fellows could tell he was interested in being a star as we watched him, at his young age, study the game. He was real easy to get along with—he was a good kid. I was more outspoken and I'd have to pick him up once in a while. He'd get down on himself because he went one for four or one for three, and I'd gone zero for four and he'd be complaining. I would say, "Hey buddy, how about me! I'm the one that's suppose to be down. I went zero for four, and you went one for three and drove in two runs. Come on kid, get your head up!"

And he would say, "I can do better than that."

I'd say, "I know you can, but take it easy on yourself." He was just that kind of kid—he just kept pushing himself to be better. I knew his potential, and when I saw his work ethics, I knew he'd be a star someday. You don't get many kids that come around often like Johnny.

What surprised me the most was the power he had for such a little guy. He was surprising. I used to come over to him and ask where he got that power. He'd just grin, and I finally figured it out by watching him. He had those quick wrists, but more important was his incredible timing. He met the ball so squarely.

I think the way the White Sox were saying he was going to be another Mickey Mantle hurt Johnny. You know, I never saw him like Mickey Mantle—Mantle belonged in a league by himself. I knew right at first he'd be a better-than-average ballplayer, and we never could figure it out why the White Sox didn't stay with him. In a year or two he would have been a great star for them because they had the guys to hit around him. But back in those days they hardly gave anyone a chance. You had to do it all right away or they'd ship you down or trade you.

I liked playing in Philadelphia. The people were really good if you hustled. They really stuck by you. If you dogged it and didn't hustle they would really get on you—they really would! If you gave it your 100 percent, no matter what you were doing out there, they would go along with you. But if you didn't, they would let you know about it—real bad!

Looking back, I think Johnny did real well. He had three or four things going for him, and any time you could hit twenty-five to thirty home runs in those days, you were doing really well. I've often thought, if Johnny would have been playing for a first division team when he first came up, he would have took off right away. If you have three or four hitters around you, they have to pitch to you. Johnny had to carry the club himself most of the time—a difficult thing to do, especially in those days.

Baseball is a different game today. Take Mantle and Aaron—they played with great ballplayers, and a lot of their success, take nothing away from them, came because they had a lot of support. In those days most teams had five or six good hitters, which wasn't true on the Phillies. Johnny had to carry the burden himself. God only knows what he might have done had he been in the Yankee, Dodgers, or Braves lineup back then. Today is the reverse; most teams have only one or two good ballplayers. If Johnny would have played today he'd fit right in. He'd still have to carry a team. Although, the kids that can play nowadays are probably better than they've ever been. Good God, some of those boys can play.

In my book Johnny was a superstar. Anyone that did what he did and lasted sixteen years in those days was a superstar even if he was a "candy-arm" at first!

*   *   *

A pall of gloom seemed to hang over Connie Mack stadium this year, and I noticed it right off. We played so poorly and most of the time there were so few people in the stands that sometimes I thought I could hear whoever was there whisper. The Phillies had given up twenty-three home runs when they'd traded me for Gene Freese, and I knew it. Trying to make the trade look good, I once again began striving to hit a home run every time I came up to bat. The pitchers would sucker me with slow curves and change-ups. Paul Waner, who was only a springtime instructor, was no longer around to help straighten me out, so I went into a hitting tailspin. My inner frustration seemed to be killing me.

Mauch played me in left field in 1960 and, for some reason, I had a difficult time picking up the ball. Most of the batters were right-handed, and when they swung through the ball, I just seemed to lose my normal jump. The fans in the left-field stands tried to get rid of me. They wanted Freese back and they were quick to tell me about it every day. They'd yell; "Send Callison back to the White Sox. Send Callison down to Buffalo." I got shipped out a hundred times. They threw money at me—pennies mostly, but once in a while I got a quarter and was really living it up. I figured, if they're going to throw money at me I may as well take it, so I'd kind of sneak it between innings. There was one stretch of home games where I must have made at least ten dollars.

But the money turned to beer cans next. They'd fire them at me. Soon, I was playing ball with one eye on the stands and one on the hitter. I remember this one guy who was always drunk. I never really got a good look at him because I was afraid to look up—as soon as I'd look up, everybody in the left-field stands would get on

70

me. But this asshole was at the park almost every day, and he'd greet me in this monstrous voice that everyone could hear all over the ball park: "Here comes that bum again." It was a big thing for me. I was only twenty-one years old and I couldn't understand why they wanted to treat me in this fashion. I guess they were right, though. They bought the tickets. And we played so poorly!

My confidence had hit its lowest ebb. I was playing with the worst team in baseball, not regularly, and I thought maybe I shouldn't be in the big leagues. This first season with the Phillies had turned into a nightmare. One thing I always had was my speed, but I knew that my injuries had permanently slowed me down at least two steps. My throwing, consequently, was erratic, and I frequently missed the cutoff man. Gene Mauch wouldn't let me play against left-handed pitchers, rationalizing that he didn't want my confidence tarnished. He was doing the wrong thing because his strategy worked in reverse with my way of thinking. I'd have a good day against a right-hander and the next day he would bench me. I would get down on myself, and my good friend Bobby Del Greco would have to kick me to pick me back up. He had ceased calling me Candy now, but his way of giving me a kick was to call me Mrs. Callison.

I became really depressed by season's end. I kept thinking about signing with the White Sox for such a token bonus. Players like Mike McCormick had signed for $50,000, and I was making a salary of slightly better than the minimum ($7,000) in Philadelphia. I was angry, although with the way things were going, I wondered if I was worth any more than what I was getting. We had purchased a house in Bakersfield, which we rented to the manager of the Bears, and we were renting a house in Philadelphia. The arithmetic wasn't adding up, and it was a difficult thing to try live like one would think a big league player should live.

God is good, and the season of 1960 ended with me playing in ninety-nine games, 288 official at bats, 9 home runs, 30 RBIs, and I hit a mere .260. I've never been one to give myself any credit, but it was a big change switching leagues. I can honestly say, in retrospect, that the National League umpires make their ball–strike calls a lot more consistently, and that was something I learned to appreciate.

The mental torture wasn't over yet, however. At season's end Dianne, Lori, and I set off on the long trip to Bakersfield. En route we had a flat tire, and because the car was rattling so much we had to pay for an alignment. At Gallup, New Mexico, we ran out of gas. Because of paying for the alignment I had only seven dollars left in my wallet. I found a Chinese restaurant where I was able to feed the entire family for three dollars. After dinner Dianne tried for hours to reach her mother on the telephone, calling collect, of course. Finally, she got ahold of her, and Babe wired money from California so her daughter, granddaughter, and big league ballplayer son-in-law could get home.

No matter how good things look in life—"Shit happens." Once in Bakersfield, I counted on finding a job to tide us over until spring training. In fact, back in those days, most players had to have a winter job to get by. Nope! There were no jobs in Bakersfield. I'll never forget having to sell our huge parrot we'd purchased the winter before in Maracaibo we'd named Herman. Herman was the most cantankerous bird you'd ever meet. He was always trying to bite me, but like I said before, I guess he was what we salvaged out of that fiasco in Venezuela and we didn't want to part with him. We had to eat, so we sold him for $100 and a few other items, like our stereo set. I was still a ballplayer, though, and I was certain I would get paid more money the coming year. But when I tried to negotiate with John Quinn he simply told me, "Johnny, I've been trying to trade you but nobody wants you." I began thinking he was probably right! On the positive side, our daughter Cindy was born in Bakersfield on December 29, 1960.

*   *   *

John Sletten:

In the spring of 1961 I was just completing my junior year of high school in Montevideo, Minnesota. It was a time of excitement for the people of Minnesota, including myself, as the winter snow was melting off with the coming of April. Why? We were waiting anxiously for the debut of major league baseball in our grand state, even if our team was the lowly and displaced Washington Senators, who were now our Minnesota Twins.

Little did anyone know then that the year 1961 would change major league baseball's hallowed structure and record books. From 1901 through 1960 baseball had managed to preserve its limited franchise sanctuary of sixteen teams. There were only 400 big league ballplayers and they were the best. Every team had at least four or five true par-excellent players, with the better teams able to field a lineup of seven or eight quality hitters. Branch Rickey, with his keen foresight, could see the talent the American and National Leagues had accumulated. Rickey began making overtures which threatened the system with his plans for a third major circuit, which he proposed to be the Continental League. However, with the increasing reach of television and jet travel shrinking the country, the American League expanded to ten teams in 1961.

When the old Washington Senators abandoned D.C. for a new home in Minneapolis, an expansion team formed in Washington as the new Senators, as did one in the increasingly popular West as the Los Angeles Angels. Remember, the Brooklyn Dodgers and the New York Giants had stolen away from Ebbets Field and the Polo Grounds for Los Angeles and San Francisco, respectively, at the end of the 1957 season. As a result of the addition of the two new teams, the American League expanded its schedule for 154 to 162 games. Fate, as it does so often, would lend its fickle hand by having Roger Maris—an unknown name, a left-handed hitter the Yankees picked up from the Kansas City A's only a year before, a youngster from Fargo, North Dakota—hit sixty-one home runs in 1961 with number sixty coming in game 159 and number sixty-one in the 162nd contest. The Babe's (George Herman Ruth) home run record of sixty in a single season (1927) had been shattered. However, there will be a forever asterisk in the baseball annals because the Bambino hit sixty in 154 ball games. The controversies were just beginning in baseball and the world.

I love baseball, and I can still remember, as clear as if it were yesterday, my dad putting an old wooden bat in my hand when I was five years old. We were in the backyard of our house on 6th Street when Dad positioned my hands on the bat and showed me how to take an effective swing. He paced off about twenty feet and tossed me my first pitch. The ball hit me squarely in the forehead and I started to cry, while my father kept telling me, "That didn't hurt!"

Through the years my dad played catch with me nearly every day after work, and as we would toss the ball back and forth, he would tell me all about the big league ballplayers past and present. On sultry summer Sundays we'd sit in front of a fan in the kitchen by the big radio to listen to the games coming from St. Louis, Milwaukee, or Chicago. It would be whichever one we could get tuned in that particular day. By the time I was twelve years old I knew every batting lineup and starting pitcher rotation for all sixteen teams. Dad was now hitting me flyballs and line drives (and he could hit) while I ran them down in a huge vacant lot. He was always trying to hit one over my head, but I don't think he ever did it. You see, his dream was for me to become a big league baseball player, and it was mine as well. Perhaps during this particular period of time it was most fathers' dearest reverie, and in most young boys' wandering imaginations.

Somewhere around that time I took my fantasy a little bit further. I put three or four dollars in an envelope and sent off for a Red Barber baseball game. When it arrived I set up a ballpark of my own in my bedroom closet. This little 4 by 4 space provided a lot of hours of fun for me when I was growing up. I put a small table against one wall and a tiny wooden desk adjacent to the table on another wall. There was just enough room left for a chair and me. I placed my game board on the table and surrounded it with newspaper clipping of fans in the stands glued on the wall. I kept meticulous statistics of all my games, and after I summarized each game I'd file the scoresheet neatly in my desk.

I had each of the teams play 25 games, which means with sixteen teams I played 200 games during the months April through September (four hundred hours). Each game, at bat, etc., I multiplied by six to equate with numbers of 150 games. Then, I'd have each team play four more games, equaling a 154-game schedule. We, of course, didn't have the luxury of calculators in those days, so Dad bought me a slide rule (showed me how to use it), and I got pretty handy with that as I accumulated all of my statistics.

But in those Red Barber games (which was controlled by a roll of dice) the stats never worked out. My best hitters were usually the worst ones in the real majors, and my World Series usually featured the Washington Senators playing the Philadelphia Phillies rather than the Yankees and the Dodgers. As I got older I saved my paper route money to buy a more sophisticated game called Big League Manager. This was a game board with a series of complicated probability charts which directly correlated with the information printed on each player's card, based on prior years' actual statistics. The game proved true to form, and the first year I used it was the 1959 season. The player's card had the 1958 season stats where Johnny Callison had just come off his great start with the White Sox. When I played my 1959 season, the White Sox won my pennant and Johnny Callison was in my lineup every day. This would be the first meeting of the ballplayer and the writer.

I'll never forget the season of 1961 because, after years of going down to Lexington Park in St. Paul with my dad in the summer to see my loves, the Brooklyn Dodgers, play a game against their Triple A farm club, the St. Paul Saints, I now had a real live major league team to root for in Minnesota. Dad, for the first time, let me drive to Minneapolis (about a hundred miles) with my girlfriend to see games at Metropolitan Stadium. It was quite a thrill, and it was then I first began to cheer for players who had once been teammates of Johnny Callison.

The Twins finished seventh their first year. Harmon Killebrew hit forty-six home runs, Billy Martin played second, Bob Allison hit twenty-nine, and we loved Earl Battey, who batted .302. Ted Lepcio and Don Mincher were there, being part of the White Sox foolishness. Camilo Pascual won 15 games; Cookie Lavagetto managed seventy-four games before Sam Mele took over. Earl Torgeson played for the Yankees, Norm Cash batted .361 for the Tigers and hit forty-one home runs driving in 132 (Bill Veeck, what a fool), Johnny Romano hit .299 for the Cleveland Indians, Barry Latman won 13 for the Tribe, Bobby Del Greco was playing with the Kansas City A's, and Johnny Callison played in 124 games, hit nine home runs, batted in forty-seven runs, and had a batting average of .266 for the Phillies.

The year 1961 was a maverick season. The world was changing and so were baseball. John Kennedy had been elected president, embarking the country on a "New Frontier." Ironically, baseball was in its "New Frontier" as well, with the addition of two new teams in the American League and a longer schedule. The sacred record of Babe Ruth was destroyed by Maris in the final game of the 162-game schedule, and the focus of America had been on the M & M boys of New York this season. Mantle hit 54 and Maris 61, eclipsing the two-man mark of 107 set by Ruth and Lou Gehrig in that record-breaking year of the Sultan of Swat in 1927. Despite the Detroit Tigers' winning 101 games this year, the Yankees won 109 to win the American League pennant, destroying Frank Robinson and the Cincinnati Reds in five games. Gene Freese had been obtained from the White Sox that year, and he hit 26 home runs batting in 87 for the Reds. Times were churning, so were baseball and Callison!

*   *   *

My second year with the Phillies was practically a duplicate of my first. I watched what Battey, Cash, and Killebrew were doing—let alone the season Gene Freese had—and I just became more depressed that I didn't belong in the Bigs! I needed more money, and when I'd try to negotiate, it was the same old story. Quinn would say, "Johnny, I've tried to trade you but nobody wants you!"

I said good-bye to Pancho, Taylor, Amaro, Charley Smith, Demeter (who we acquired from the Dodgers), Gonzalez, Dalrymple, and a host of others, including Frank Sullivan (who had served up my first hit), and called it a season. We finished last again (47–107). During this year we lost twenty-three straight games (still a record), and there were some guys on the team like Robin Roberts, Sullivan, Lee Walls, and Elmer Valo that had never been through a thing like that before. Oh, how I began to long for those glory days of my youth.

Before the end of the 1961 season Dianne and I had decided that we'd stay in Philadelphia for the winter. However, when I tried to find employment, no one would give me a job. I guess no one wanted a .266 hitter with only nine home runs around. Disillusioned, we loaded up the car and drove to Bakersfield.

During the winter I had plenty of time to think and became determined to make it this year. The National League had expanded to ten teams, adding the Houston Colt 45's and the New York Mets. At least it was encouraging that we wouldn't end up in last place 1962, and it wasn't only because of the expansion teams. We had a lot of young guys coming back that had potential, including myself—a nucleus. There would be Roy Sievers, Tony Taylor, Don Demeter, Tony Gonzalez, Clay Dalrymple, Wes Covington, Frank Torre, Ruban Amaro, Bobby Wine, and myself (Wine and I were the youngest at age twenty-three). We had some quality pitchers coming back, as well, in Art Mahaffey, Jack Baldschun, Chris Short, and Dennis Bennett. I was determined to quit sulking about the White Sox and become a Phillie. I went to spring training with a positive attitude.

However, when I reported to spring training in 1962 I couldn't believe it as Gene Mauch ignored me. I mean, he didn't act like I even existed. I tried to figure it out, but nothing made any sense. For two years he had been hounding me: "Quit trying to hit home runs. Start hitting to the opposite field so the pitchers will quit throwing to you outside." I wondered why he wasn't yelling at me this year. I hadn't changed and he hadn't changed. He was hollering at the other guys—just not me. I became worried. For two years I'd been sick of listening to him harp, and now I missed it. I began to feel alone and as if nobody cared about me this year. I began thinking that maybe they were going to trade me or, worse yet, maybe I was through already.

No one said anything to me, so I concluded I better really start working to prove to them what I could really do in case they hadn't noticed. I also began to reflect on what had happened the past two years. I had been sulking—feeling sorry for myself. I had made it clear that I didn't want to be with the Phillies. I had probably given off the impression that I was a White Sox and a White Sox is classier than a Phillie. I never said that, but I was sure now that I'd implied these notions. Now I was really worried! I began to wonder if I'd alienated myself from the club. I mean, not even Gene Mauch had anything to shout at me about. With this speculation and conjecture roaring through my mind like a freight train, I went right to work. I never worked as diligently at baseball as I did during spring training of 1962. It was up to me now, and I knew it. I figured that was the way Gene Mauch was looking at the situation as well.

One of the first things I did was pick up a forty-ounce bat—a monster of a bat—discarding my usual lightweight ones. The purpose was to shorten my swing. I didn't pull a ball all spring as I tried to hit to the opposite field. Not once did I ever try to hit a home run. I worked on my fielding and especially my throwing from the outfield. I worked so hard that spring that when training was over, I felt I was at the top of my game. But even as hard as I worked, when the season opened the New Answer, a kid named Ted Savage, who had had a good year at Buffalo the year before, had my position. They just gave it to him—I was confused.

So, I opened the season as a bench-warming pinch hitter. I kept my mouth shut, but was fuming on the inside as I watched Ted Savage play with such, in my opinion, mediocrity. But I took it, and when I got my chance I did my job. It wasn't too long before I was put into a game against Houston to pinch hit. It was a game situation and I delivered a clutch hit to win the game. I could tell right then I'd won back the affection of Gene Mauch.

I had been working with Roger Hornsby. He, of course, was one of the best hitters of all time. In more than 8,000 at bats he carried a lifetime batting average of .358. He hit 301 home runs and drove in 1,584 runs. He was an ornery sort, but he helped me a lot. He told me not to squeeze the bat so tightly. "Relax kid," he'd say. "Just go up there and relax—hitting is suppose to be fun." He was right, just like Paul Waner, and in a game against the Mets I went four for four. Gene Mauch then gave me the job of right fielder, which I kept for good. This was the beginning of good things to come. By year's end our team would finish with 81 wins against 80 loses. We finished seventh, but remember, there were now ten teams in our league and not eight. We won 34 more games than we did the year before, and I had finally arrived.

I accomplished a major goal, batting an even .300 in 1962. I hit 23 home runs (without trying to hit any) and batted in 83. I made the 1962 all-star team and hit a single off a former teammate with the White Sox, Dick Donavan. Gene Mauch was still looking at me, though. He wanted to leave my confidence peaking at season's end. When I looked at the lineup for the last game of the season I noticed I hadn't been penciled in. When I approached Mauch he was quick to say, "I want you to think of yourself as .300 hitter during the winter." I shrugged my shoulders, thinking, *I didn't hit .300 in one game. I had 603 official at bats, scored 107 runs, hit 26 doubles, and led the league in triples with 10.* Tony Gonzalez batted .302, Dom Demeter hit .307, and Frank Torre batted .310 in

76 games. Art Mahaffey won 19 games. The 1962 Phillies were coming, and so was Johnny Callison.

The New York Yankees won the pennant again; however, they were given a good chase by the two American League expansion teams—the Minnesota Twins, who finished 91–71, with Killebrew hitting 48 home runs and Camilo Pascual winning 20 games. The Los Angeles Angels, who won 86 and lost 76, had the big bats coming from Leon Wagner and Lee Thomas. Dean Chance won 14 games.

Walter O'Malley opened his baseball emporium, Dodger Stadium, for the start of the 1962 season, where they drew a record 2.7 million fans. The Dodgers got off to a quick start, pacing the National League all summer featuring Maury Wills (MVP as he broke Ty Cobb's record of stolen bases held since 1915), who stole 104 sacks, Tommy Davis (hit .346 with 153 RBIs), and the Cy Young Award pitching of Don Drysdale (25 wins). However, on July 17, ace southpaw Sandy Koufax was lost for the season with a circulatory ailment in his fingers. In the final thirteen contests, the Dodgers lost ten while the San Francisco Giants won seven to tie the Dodgers at the completion of the regular season. A one-game playoff found the Giants winning easily behind former White Sox ace Billy Pierce's three-hitter. Of course, the Yankees won the World Series four games to three. It was a hell of a year!

* * *

Dianne Callison:

Johnny batted .300 and everybody wanted him to work for them in the off season. He had job offers coming from everywhere—after the 1961 season he couldn't find a job. He listened to everyone to try and determine what he might like to do, and what he didn't like he passed on to some of his teammates. He finally accepted a job with Fleischmann's Bakery at 21st and Arch Street, where he worked two days a week as a sales representative.

The other five days of the week he managed the Broad-Olney Lanes. In his spare moments he would speak occasionally at a banquet and get some workouts in some gym. Johnny has always been so modest, and I'm certain he will always be that way, but after the 1962 season he realized that everyone was recognizing him. I think this was a big transition for him. Everyone likes to be recognized, but Johnny only wanted it to go so far. He never wanted it to get to the point where he couldn't do what he wanted or go where he wanted.

As for me, my hands were full taking care of the two girls and with household chores. Yet even with Lori, four, and Cindy, seventeen months, I remained a totally dedicated baseball wife. I loved baseball even before I met Johnny. Now, my husband was a major leaguer and I didn't want to miss any of it. I took the girls to every Sunday home game. When I wasn't at the game, I had it tuned in on the radio or television. I never went to bed until the last out, even when they were on the West Coast. I had all of the Philadelphia newspapers delivered to our house, wherever we were, to see what was written about the team and Johnny. I was always so interested in Johnny's performance.

We were still living in the Walnut Park Plaza along with the Don Demeters, Ted Savages, Billy Smiths, and Bobby Wines. The Demeters, Savages, and Smiths had two children each, and the Wines were expecting their first. I remember one evening when the wives gathered in our living room for a baby shower for the new Wine vintage, due in a week or two. We had the game on the radio, but there was so much gabbing that I didn't catch the final score— that bothered me!

I always had the game tuned in on the radio when I was home alone with the children. If the team was at home, I'd wait for Johnny to come in from a night game to tell me how the team really did, how he felt. Most of the time it was long past midnight, but I'd enjoy talking about the baseball.

Baseball life was difficult, especially at first. I guess what kept me going was just knowing I was married to someone special and that someday we would make it because I always believed in Johnny. We had been sweethearts since our junior year at East Bakersfield High, where he was the school's hero in baseball, football, and basketball.

*　　*　　*

I have always had an obstinate streak in me. I guess I was a rockhead. I remember going to Peanuts Lowery during the spring of 1962, when everyone was ignoring me, and asking him if they were going to trade me. He didn't know, and if he did, he wasn't going to tell me. So, I did it on my own and had the big year I'd always thought I'd have every year, including playing right field skillfully enough to lead the league in assists with 24. I remember running the sprints so hard it hurt me to breathe, and then I'd stop, thinking I could get myself in shape now, partly because I just didn't enjoy somebody telling me what to do. As a result, I learned a lot during the 1962 season about hitting, pitching, and conditioning myself. If the bat got heavy and my hands got slow, I learned not to panic, and rush out and take extra batting practice. I found out that this type of solution made it worse, and I learned I had to just rest when this happened.

With a budding, needing family, all my prior season work and the results thereof paid off in 1962. This time I told Quinn what I wanted (not ask), and he didn't faint or tell me how he'd been trying to trade me to no avail. I was moving and I knew it! It was with this momentum that I went into the 1963 baseball season.

As if hitting wasn't tough enough, the year 1963 included the expansion of the batter's strike zone. But it didn't seem to matter this spring. I felt as if I was an established big leaguer. I looked forward to the spring knowing I wouldn't have to bust a gut trying to win a job. For the first time I felt relaxed. I wasn't taking things for granted, nor did I intend to work less hard than I did before. But it was nice to be able to concentrate on my hitting and outfielding without worrying about somebody running me out of the lineup. It was a pleasurable spring, and Gene Mauch didn't seem to find fault with my free-and-easy attitude. He just told me he hoped I wouldn't forget how much sweat and toil I'd put in to get me where I was.

The spring before, I was concerned whether I could be playing regularly for the Phillies or some other team; now I was being touted as the man most likely to become the outstanding regular of the future. In 1962 I batted second in the batting order most of the time. We had picked up a veteran during the off season in Don Hoak, and Mauch had him slated for the second spot, moving me down to the third position. Batting third had always been the best for me, and given this opportunity, I looked forward to batting in at least 100 runs.

In 1962 I had quit fiddling with my stance and had hit .300. During my first two years with the Phillies I hit well at times, but then I would always run into at least one disastrous slump that kept my average in the .260s. But in 1962 I came out of such skids more quickly. I guess my confidence was partly responsible. Before, when I went a couple of days without a hit, I'd worry about it so much I couldn't sleep at night. I'd take extra batting practice, so much my hands would be all blisters. But in 1962 I was more able to handle a slump. I realized that everybody had them, but that worrying about them only made them worse. I stopped taking extra batting practice because it didn't seem to help, and it just took that much more out of me by the time it came to play the game.

Bunts helped! A lot of times I would get in a streak where I was hitting the ball well, but it went right at somebody. That's how most of my slumps started in the past, and then I'd start worrying about them. Not any more. I would bunt for a hit now and then, and it kept me from going into slumps where I wouldn't get a hit for a week. My goals for 1963 were to improve on each of last year's figures. Most of all I wanted to get over one hundred RBIs.

But with all that, the season got off to a poor start—I was trying too hard again. On the fourth of June I was hitting a lowly .222, with everyone thinking I should be battling the National League leaders. "Hang in there!" I got so sick of hearing that advice. Every time I came back to the bench after failing to get a base hit, my teammates offered me the customary sympathy. In the past it worked, but I didn't want sympathy anymore—I wanted hits. I became impatient. I just wasn't snapping out of it like I did in 1962. Simply, I figured, I was trying too hard. I wasn't picking up the ball well after it left the pitcher's hand. I couldn't understand why. What bothered me the most was I was hurting the club. But this year Gene Mauch was hanging in with me like I was a seasoned veteran—I appreciated his confidence and it had a lot to do with pulling me out of it.

But I kept fighting myself, and Mauch made overtures that he was not going to bench me but give me a rest instead. I protested. I wanted to battle it out myself, and he said, "Okay you might as well start battling."

On June 28, 1963, we were playing Pittsburgh and I broke out of my slump in a big way. I hit for the cycle for the third time in my career (it hasn't been done since by a Phillie, as of this writing). This was the first time I did it in the Bigs, but I had done it once before during that first summer with the Bakersfield Bears. I also did it that first year with Indianapolis against the Minneapolis Millers. I tripled in the first inning, scoring the first run; then, swinging like I'd never been in a slump, I clouted the longest home run of my career. I hit a Don Cardwell fastball over the fifteen-foot gate in right center. Only three other guys had done that, I found out later: Duke Snider, Dale Long, and Bill Terry. My next at bat I singled and then connected with a run-producing double. Ironically, that same game, Tony Gonzalez committed his first error in 205 games; it was a major league record at the time.

For some reason Richie Ashburn, former great Phillies center fielder, who was in his freshman year as a Philadelphia announcer, pitched batting practice. After we won that first game with Pittsburgh, Gene asked Richie to pitch batting practice again and again as we swept that series. After the third game someone asked Richie if he was going to keep throwing batting practice. Ashburn replied, "I don't want any credit, but as long as the team keeps on winning, I'll keep throwing."

During a three-week stint we won 13 out of 16 games and 20 of 27, if you included the 9 games prior to the run. We were playing at a .740 clip and it wasn't a fluke. For some reason we just started playing the kind of ball we were capable of playing. Roy Sievers had finally recovered from ailing ribs; Don Hoak and I had broken out of our slumps. The pitching had been good all year long, and now our fielding had reached the point where our defense was at an equal to that of any team in the league. It had been poor hitting from the gate in 1963, leaving runners stranded all of the time. During our winning stretch we compiled a team batting average of .312.

The team was starting to form. For the second straight year it took us half a season to get moving, but as mid-July approached we felt we were as tough a team to beat as there was in the National League. We had legs, gloves, arms, and finally bats at every position. We had infielders who were now playing infield. We had enough pitchers available to allow our only early season stopper, Ray Culp, extra time to rest his elbow. Hoak and Sievers were solid at the corners of the infield, Wine and Amaro platooned at short, and Tony Taylor was hot at second. Earlier in the season, when Sievers was ailing and Hoak was slumping, Don Demeter, our regular center fielder, was alternating between first and third. Now he was back in center, Gonzalez was back in left, and I was in right. When Demeter was playing third or first, Wes Covington played left and Gonzalez played center. Our defense was hurting then as Demeter was an outfielder, not an infielder, and although Covington always swung a good bat, he was heavy-legged, making him suspect on defense. We were strong up the middle as well, with strong-armed Clay Dalrymple behind the plate and Tony Taylor at second.

Dennis Bennett, about this time, had recovered from an off-season auto accident injury. We salvaged relief ace John Boozer from the minors, and Dallas Green seemed to find what he had a year ago. Art Mahaffey was finding his stride to help Culp, who had carried the starting rotation from the beginning of the season. No, we were no longer a mirage, instead, a real bona fide team on the come and looking for a pennant.

On Tuesday, July 16, 1963, Connie Mack Stadium was jammed with some 35,000 fans. It was reported the next day more than 20,000 had been turned away. It was exciting and this was baseball like I thought it would be once I got to the Bigs. I was becoming very confident in myself, and it seemed like I was hitting left-handers better than I was right-handers. I had moved my average to .279 and our team was 45–47—eleven and a half games out of first place, although we were still in eighth place.

Before the Pittsburgh series I had told manager Gene Mauch that I'd been jerking my head off the ball and I'd been thinking too much. I told him I didn't know if I could break the slump but I knew sitting on the bench wasn't the way. He listened to me and I started to perform. On this day against the Dodgers, in the second game of a double header, I went four for four. Sandy Koufax beat us in the first game 5–2. After you face Koufax, anyone who follows looks like they're throwing a grapefruit at you. Nick Willhite threw the second game, and he never got anyone out. I singled off him, homered off reliever Ed Roebuck, homered off left-hander Dick Scott, and singled off right-hander Larry Sherry.

In the first game I got a bunt single off Koufax, so I wound up five for eight and boosted my average to near .300 after going fourteen for thirty in eight exciting games with the Giants and the Dodgers. Mauch told me he had a lot of theories as to why this big turnaround happened, but what made me feel good was when he said, ".300 hitters hit .300, whether they start from .150 or .450."

On Sunday, August 25, 1963, we were battling Pittsburgh before a big crowd at Connie Mack in the bottom of the eleventh inning when ace reliever Elroy Face served up a fastball which I picked up on and smashed out of the park for my nineteenth home run and a game winner. I remember a reporter saying to me after the game, "You and everyone else knew it was gone as soon as you hit it."

I replied, "Did I?" I had started to become a little more brash and it felt good, mostly because I was going good—so was the team.

A strange thing happened during that game. As we took the field in the bottom of the fourth inning, a band of Cubans raced onto the field. They were carrying flags and signs and they first encircled Tony Gonzalez and then visited Tony Taylor before police ran them out of the ballpark. I don't know to this day what it was all about, but it was kind of scary. Only a year before, Kennedy had run those missiles out of Cuba and I wondered about that. Nothing came of it! Gonzalez and Taylor were both Cubans, and I'm glad that band of crazies visited them rather than me.

On September 25, 1963, we beat the Giants, leaving us within one game of third place. I hit my twenty-fifth home run of the year off of Don Larsen (1956 perfect game in the Series) to seal the victory. After the game Gene Mauch looked at me and said with a smile, "Every good hitter just needs his time in the sun."

*   *   *

Clay Dalrymple:

I remember just looking at Johnny when he first came to spring training in 1960. I wondered how this kid, so small in stature, was going to be the power hitter they were rating him to be. Hell, he only weighed 170 pounds and stood about five foot ten. I would soon find out, however, they were right. Johnny had excellent power and it all came from his hands and forearms. He had very strong arms, and he would turn out to be our power hitter as predicted.

Johnny was always quiet and never caused a problem on the team. He reminded me of the stereotype of a good old southern boy. He moved kind of slow and was very easygoing. In his spare time he liked to bowl, and when we were on the road he liked to go to movies or just sit around talking and laughing. He wasn't a teetotaler but he didn't drink like some of the guys did back then. I often thought that he was too dedicated an athlete to abuse himself in that way.

In 1961 I became the regular catcher—I caught 122 games that year, going through the hell of being part of the record-breaking twenty-three-game losing streak. It was a pretty stressful situation for us all. When we'd lost fourteen or fifteen in a row it seemed pretty bad, but when we got up into the twenties it really became hard to deal with.

One time, during our record breaking losing streak Mauch went on a tirade in Houston. There was no place worse in baseball to play than in Houston before the Astrodome was built, and their club was known as the Colt 45's. The old stadium was cut right out of a cow pasture. Every inning, when you'd come in from the field you had to spray the bugs off your clothing and body. The heat was stifling.

On that day, each inning we'd come in complaining about the bugs and the heat, when finally Mauch screamed out, "I'm sick of your griping about the climate and the insects—they have to play in it, too—next guy who complains about anything gets fined a hundred bucks!"

The next inning, Johnny returned from the outfield sweating and covered with bugs. He flopped down on the bench and groaned, "God is it ever hot out there!" Everyone looked at him, before he remembered Mauch's recent admonition. Very quickly Johnny said, "Good'n hot, just the way I like it!"

We all laughed and so did Mauch. Gene said, "Funny how quickly a guy can think when there's a hundred dollars on the line!"

I'll never forget when it ended. I got the game-winning hit off

Carlton Willey against Milwaukee to end the streak. This feat was the only argument I had to negotiate my 1962 contract because everything else in 1961 had gone so horseshit.

Gene Mauch, Johnny, and I all started together in 1960, and everything (most everything) that has been said about Gene since was true. He was a fiery little guy and, at that time, the youngest major league manager ever. As a ballplayer he only played in 304 games and for a variety of teams. His lifetime average was a meek .239. But I've always thought the ballplayers who had limited ability, like Gene, paid more attention to the game itself, trying to get that certain edge. Gene studied the game real hard and turned out to be an excellent manager, getting more out of a player perhaps than the player would have gotten out of himself. As for a superstar, things just come too easy for them. They don't have to study the game because their natural ability just takes over. Of course, there are guys like Gene, who have that certain ability to notice all the little things about the game or a player that make the big things turn out like they were meant to be.

I think Gene Mauch was responsible for Johnny reaching his full potential. He made him work and Johnny did work. He was always out there taking extra batting practice. I can say this, too. I think Johnny really just loved the game of baseball. He had been heralded as the next Mickey Mantle by the White Sox, and I think that was a hell of a bad thing for them to do to a nineteen-year-old boy. Nobody could be a Mickey Mantle, really. He was one of a kind and had thirty or forty pounds on Johnny. Mickey was much stronger, plain and simple. Johnny had the greatest, quickest swing, though, that I ever saw. And had he played with some strong clubs during his career, he would have hit .300 and hit 25 or 30 home runs probably every year. I truly believe this. In fact, my theory was proved when Richie Allen came up in 1964. The pitchers had to pitch to Johnny because Dick Allen was next. Baseball is a tough racket, and one's success can be measured so much by the team and players you play with. It is a difficult, difficult thing to play 162 ball games. You get up, go to the ballpark, play the game, go to the whirlpool to soothe an aching body, go home to bed, and get up and do the whole deal over again day after day. The season itself can lull you to sleep unless there is something extra going for you that stirs the adrenaline of a great athlete. Mostly that extra something can be attributed to winning. If you're not winning, it's difficult keeping motivated day after day after day.

I think Johnny was a superstar. In Philadelphia I know he was for sure. As a ballplayer he could steal a base for you, he had an excellent arm, he'd get you a lot of extra base hits, and he'd hit his twenty home runs or so. More importantly, he was a team leader. A team leader to me is not a cheerleader. My idea of a team leader is a reliable person who gets along with his teammates, and when the team needs a hit—the team leader will get it for you. Johnny always would get you the big hit. Johnny was a team leader!

I was back in Philadelphia on August nineteenth for the reunion of the 1964 Phillies. I took a trip out to 21st and Lehigh with a writer doing an article for the occasion. When we arrived I became kind of nostalgic. I remembered the great days on that square block of vacant land—days I wouldn't trade for all the money in the world. And there was no money playing baseball in those days—it was just a hell of an experience.

I remembered the great fans and great players I shared those days with. In my reminiscing I stood at the corner of 21st and Lehigh and paced off 135 steps diagonally. I stopped right there, being certain I was within ten feet of where home plate once was stationed. "Where were the stands?" I imagined someone might ask, as only the sidewalk remains on the perimeter of that hallowed ground. I would say they were once right on the sidewalk, going straight up, with the top deck being built on top of the lower deck. I looked to my right and I could still see that huge fence right where there were no stands. Connie Mack had put that fence up so people who lived in the area couldn't watch the games from their house. I peered into center field where I envisioned the huge scoreboard with the Ballantine Beer sign speaking proudly. Then I looked toward the left where there were stands from center to the corner and all down the line. The place where they hounded Johnny, at first, and on top of the roof I could still see that Coca-Cola sign. I'll never forget, watching in amazement, when Dick Allen sent one in orbit well over the landmark—must have hit it 600 feet or more. Yes, it was once a great ballpark, and it was home for Johnny and me for ten years.

*   *   *

After a poor start, we had made a hell of a run for the National League pennant, falling twelve games short of the Los Angeles Dodgers. We won sixteen more games than we did in 1962, giving us a respectable record of 87–75, and we finished in fourth place only one game behind the third-place San Francisco Giants. Playing slightly above .500 ball, our team neither won nor lost consistently. Our longest winning streak was eight games and the longest losing streak was five. July was our hot month. I batted .321, Gonzalez hit .357, Roy Sievers batted .302. Tony Taylor hit .302 in May and .326 in August. Taylor hit .368 against the Reds pitching, I hit the New York Mets at .346, and Gonzalez feasted for .356 against Houston hurlers. Roy Sievers found the best pitching in the league, the Los Angeles Dodgers (team ERA 2.86), his special meat, hitting Koufax and company for a .346 average. Don Demeter hit .356 against the Cardinals. So, our team balanced each other out against different club pitching. And as a team, we finished third in team hitting with .252, second in team fielding with .978, and fourth in pitching ERA of 3.11.

The season of 1963 had me playing 157 games. I batted for an average of .284, 36 doubles, 11 triples, 26 home runs, and I drove in 78 runs. I also scored 96 runs.

The Dodgers beat the Yankees four straight in the series with their remarkable pitching. Sandy Koufax won the MVP and the Cy

Young Award by winning 25 games during the regular season, and he also won two World Series games.

Pete Rose played his rookie year with the Reds and batted a cool .273, recording his first 170 hits. Harmon Killebrew hit 45 round-trippers to lead the American League again. Don Mincher and Earl Battey combined with 43 more, making the Minnesota Twins a viable contender for a 1964 pennant, thanks to the Chicago White Sox. And Norm Cash, another White Sox former mate, slapped 26 home runs for the Tigers.

I still thought about Harm, Don, Earl, and Norm and what might have been had we all stuck together. But I was happy to be a Phillie now, and I could see with the guys we had 1964 might be the year.

Chapter Five

Callison for President

Courage is the virtue that President Kennedy most admired. He sought out those people who had demonstrated in some way, whether it was on a battlefield or a baseball diamond in a speech or fighting for a cause, that they would stand up, that they could be counted on.
    —Robert F. Kennedy
      In his foreword to the Memorial Edition of his brother John
      Fitzgerald Kennedy's book *Profiles in Courage*
      December 18, 1963

I hated Gene Mauch at first. He was a real cocky type of guy, and I remembered him when I played for Indianapolis. He managed the Minneapolis Millers and everybody loved to beat him. He was hot-tempered, fiery, and acid-tongued. He couldn't have possessed a more different personality than mine as his anger struck outwardly, while I harbored mine within my intestines. But here we were beginning our fifth season with the Philadelphia Phillies together, and my hatred for him had turned to respect.

We complemented each other, however. Mauch had little ability as a ballplayer but he made the most of a quick mind and a burning desire to succeed. On the other hand, I had all the athletic ability, except great size, with the gift of timing, speed, and muscle which might have been wasted without Gene's direction. It has been said that without Mauch I would have always struggled, never capitalizing on my talent. And, without me, Mauch might have never put together a winning team while in a Philadelphia uniform.

Who knows what would've have happened, but in my eyes he was the man who most influenced my major league career. It was during the winter of 1964 when I began appreciating how much he had done for me. During our first four years we shared together the bitter taste of defeat and failure matured the both of us. He stuck to his principles and I acquiesced to working his program. Slowly, I began to accept his advice, which included not going for the long ball, platooning against left-handers, and learning to think defensively. I also learned how to hit to left field. It was a big thing for me to listen to him because I knew he'd never been a good ballplayer. What I didn't realize is that he knew the game and I didn't. I quit trying to kill the ball and pull it each time I was at bat. Gene kept his faith in me, and, when I started playing the game his way, I became a ballplayer who could compete successfully on a major league level.

Gene used to say, "The pitchers who keep the ball down and away on you, John, are tough to pull. If you can just learn to go into the ball against those pitchers and hit it to left, your average can go way up. Listen, I can make you a more valuable player and you can make more money that way then you can by trying to pull everything. Listen, if I thought you were capable of batting 35 or 40 home runs I wouldn't try to change you, you have good power, but it's not that good, and our ball park is against you. . . . "

I guess Gene was just smarter than me because he could tell, at first, that I was hearing what he said—just not listening. He never gave up and kept working with me on hitting to left, bunting, base running, and fielding. It took a couple of years, but in 1962 and 1963 something had rubbed off because I was beginning to meet my expectations.

I had ripened as we readied to embark on the 1964 season. I was prouder of the less spectacular things I did to win games versus juicing an unimportant home run. I began to take pride in my ability to hit behind a runner when the occasion called for such a maneuver, to bunt, to execute the delayed steal, and to do the other things which weren't often reflected on the front page of the newspaper. But what I was doing helped pull our team out of the cellar and into a difficult team to beat. I took a lot of pride in my outfielding. Peanuts Lowrey spent many an hour with me in the outfield, and in 1962 not only did I bat .300, I'd turned, almost overnight, into a top-flight fielder after being shifted from left to right. More important was my throwing. I remember the first time I threw a man out at the plate to save a game, and I was mystified by the gasps of the fans. In 1962 I led the league in assists from the outfield, and many attributed this to the fact that my sudden improvement had caught runners by surprise. In 1963, though, I led the league again with even more assists and people started to believe—so did I.

I always had a strong arm, but when I came to the Phillies I didn't know how to use it. I was seldom in position to make a good throw. Gene was always looking for an advantage, and with Lowrey's tutelage, I always seemed to be in the right position to make a deceiving throw. I truly believe the development of my fielding and throwing skills rounded me out as a complete major league ballplayer.

About Peanuts Lowrey! He was a little guy, only five foot eight and 170 pounds. He played for several National League teams during his career, including Cincinnati, Chicago, St. Louis, and Philadelphia. In more than 4,300 official at bats he hit a respectable .273. He hit right and threw right. He was an excellent outfielder and he taught me a lot. He was a nice guy, and I owe him my success at becoming a good major league outfielder.

Gene told me just before the 1964 campaign began, "I don't know if you'll ever lead the league in batting or home runs or in stealing bases or fielding, but you can do more things well than all but a few, and you're only twenty-five."

*   *   *

Bobby Wine:

I came up with the Phillies organization in 1957. I wasn't as talented as Johnny so by 1960 I was still bouncing back and forth between Buffalo and Philadelphia. But I sure do remember him when he first came up at the time. We were in spring training together in 1960. Right off, I thought he was a pretty good ballplayer. He had a great swing and not an overly strong arm but an accurate one. I was just a kid then, too, and trying to make it, but I noticed that he really had what it took.

I didn't see that much of Johnny during 1960 and 1961; like I said, I was too busy traveling between Buffalo and Philadelphia. I kept my eye on what was going on, of course, and in my opinion Johnny was making great progress, even if he didn't think so. He was a consistent .260 hitter (hell, that would make you a three-million-dollar-a-year man today), played good outfield, and could steal you a base. However, he had in his mind that he was supposed to be a star right away and kept fighting himself and Gene Mauch.

Through it all, the Phillies were trying to rebuild, and in his first two years they still had a lot of older ballplayers on the team; he made his mark. In 1962 I made that team to stay and Johnny took off—he'd finally arrived in his mind, too. I've always said that it just took time for Johnny to learn the pitchers. Baseball is a tough game, and during his third year he found out how they were going to pitch him. Actually, it is an incredible feat to ever solve this problem unless you have incredible talent, which Johnny possessed.

Johnny would bitch about Mauch platooning him and this or that, but what he didn't realize was Gene took care of him. Most of the guys had a roommate. Johnny roomed by himself. Mauch played a psychological game with Callison, trying to figure out what would make him maximize his ability. I don't think anyone ever figured it out, but by the time I was up to stay, Johnny was one of the best ballplayers in the game.

Funny, Johnny ended up taking care of me when I first came up to stay in 1962. He told me where they lived and helped me secure an apartment at the Walnut Park Plaza, where he and his family dwelled. We became good friends and hung out together when we were on the road. We liked the same things—movies and just talking. I'd just gotten married that year and I was pretty suited to be a family man like Johnny.

I had played well in 1963; in fact, I had the second best fielding percentage (.971) of National League shortstops. Some said I had the strongest arm among my peers, and I went into the 1964 season as optimistic as I had ever been. The year before, I'd chalked up 359 assists and 220 put-outs. I was ready, and I knew my teammate and friend, Johnny Callison, would be the main link in the chain if we were going to make our move this year.

*   *   *

John Sletten:

The year 1964 was to become the most memorable season ever played at 21st and Lehigh. At first it was called Shibe Park. The Philadelphia Athletics (American League) moved in there on April 12, 1909, the Monday after Easter.

Shibe Park was the first steel-and-concrete plant ever built as a ballpark, and it contained thirty thousands seats. Opening day it exceeded that capacity. Horses and buggies and derby hats were the order in those days for spectators. The original dimensions of the playing field were 360 down the foul line and 393 in the power alleys and 420 to dead center field.

In 1913 Shibe Park (Ben Shibe was a minor stockholder in the Athletics of the nineteenth century and a close friend of A. J. Reach, a successful sporting goods manufacturer and retailer who had determined that there was greater profit in a new, more commodious ballpark and put one at Broad and Lehigh) underwent its first major renovation when the uncovered stands were roofed over and a left-field stand was added, extending to the center-field flagpole.

In 1925 a second deck was constructed from behind first base to the right-field corner, and from behind third base to left field and on to dead center field. For twenty-five years, the right-field wall was only twelve feet high. The situation invited competition from 20th Street property owners who built bleachers on their rooftops and sold tickets at bargain rates. In 1935 the wall was raised to fifty feet, putting the wildcat operators out of business. This was the Philadelphia Athletics park at 21st and Lehigh. The aforementioned in parentheses at Broad and Lehigh was known as Huntington Grounds and later as the Baker Bowl when it collapsed and hurled 200 spectators onto Huntington Street. The owner was William F. Baker. This was May 27, 1927, when the Phillies were playing the St. Louis Cardinals. In 1938 the last game at the Baker Bowl was played, and the Phillies moved to Shibe Park at the invitation of Connie Mack.

Shibe Park introduced night baseball to the American League on May 16, 1939. Two all-star games were played at Shibe on July 13, 1943, when Bobby Doerr's home run won it for the American League. On July 8, 1952, in a game shortened to five innings by rain, the National League won 3–2 by collecting only three hits, but two were home runs hit by Jackie Robinson and Hank Sauer.

For years Connie Mack had resisted suggestions that the park be renamed in his honor. But in 1952, when Mack was in Florida, the board of directors voted to make the change. The A's departed for Kansas City in 1954, and the Phillies bought the stadium for an estimated $2 million.

So, Shibe Park, also known as Connie Mack Stadium in honor of the man who managed the Athletics for fifty years, was baseball's first steel-and-concrete park. Its front entrance was at the corner of 21st and Lehigh in North Philadelphia.

*   *   *

Bobby Wine:

Connie Mack was a romantic ballpark. The entrance was domed at the corner of 21st and Lehigh, with two names displayed above the center gate. SHIBE PARK—CONNIE MACK STADIUM.

It looked like a fortress on the outside. Inside, however, it was home. It was a great place to play. It always gave me a warm feeling as the natural grass seemed to just blow with the wind. The infield was fine, and each spectator's wooden seat made them seem like they were sitting right across from you at the Thanksgiving table. The stands were closed along the lines, although there was plenty of foul territory. In right field there was only a wall, and as you moved to right center field there was a huge scoreboard advertising Ballantine Beer. There was a Longines clock atop that. From dead center to the left-field corner there were two tiers of stands. High atop were the Coca-Cola and Philco signs. For a modern-day ballplayer, well, they would've died. It was a bad neighborhood (the racial riots were just beginning in 1964), nowhere to park (twenty-five cents buddy, watch your car), and the clubhouse was crude. The dugout was half of what the players have now, and the clubhouse had a cold concrete floor. We had five showers and you just took your turn. Above the dressing room was a balcony where the minor medical miracles were performed to put crippled players into shape to play. Our trainer, Joe Liscio, would try to heal our pulled muscles and spike wounds. There were sun lamps, rubbing tables, weights, diathermy machine, whirlpool baths, and scores of bottles of pills and ointments. If someone was seriously injured the team physician, Dr. K. George Laquer, took over. It is different now, but it was wonderful then, and I wished we could have kept it that simple.

*   *   *

On Saturday, April 4, 1964, a few of us from the Phillies and a contingent from other American and National League teams gathered at a bowling alley in Tampa for a "Basebowl" put on by the Brunswick Corporation. I guess in those days it proved that you could get a $20,000-a-year baseball player anywhere if you provided him a ride, free beer, a game of chance, and a shot at a few hundred bucks. Most of the ballplayers were not good bowlers, and I think Clay Dalrymple said it best: "I could have rolled my mitt down there and done better!"

After a few games, to determine the best from each league, the final event came, featuring the top ten from the National League to roll off against the top ten from the American League. Each of us was to roll one frame. I guess I had an advantage, having worked at the Broad-Olney Lanes during the off season—I was always a good bowler, though. But I've never seen such poor bowling. I was the anchor for our team, and when I came up in the tenth frame we were behind. Gene Mauch was observing; when it was my turn, he shouted, "Men on base, last of the ninth."

I rolled three balls and struck out. Bang! Bang! Bang! We won. National League 137 and the American League 101. Little did I know this insignificant event would be a portent of a significant episode to come as the 1964 baseball campaign was now about to get under way.

Inside, I was still worrying I guess. I was only comfortable when I had a bat or ball in my hand. After a couple of good years I was receiving opportunities to peddle products on television, model clothes, and the people were telling me I had the good looks to do movies. I laughed all of this kind of stuff off, not really believing people were being serious with their overtures of fortune. I knew I was the right fielder for the Phillies, that we had a pretty good team going into 1964, and during the off season I liked working on sales for the bakery. Beyond all of that I still possessed a near-shy personality that people had been trying to tamper with from the time baseball scouts were knocking at my door in East Bakersfield.

Gene Mauch had never tried to convert my personality or force leadership responsibilities on me. I would say to people, when asked, "I'm no superstar. Maybe I never will be, but as long as I get on base often the club seems to go better. That's all I'm interested in—keeping the club moving."

Just before the 1964 season began, however, I read in the paper where Mauch had said, "Of all the players on this team, Johnny's got the best chance to be a superstar. And everybody will look to him for leadership."

Thank God, Gene qualified his remarks when he said "chance."

I was more confident now, however. The past season Houston's Hal Woodeshick struck me out nine of ten times. For the first time, I had told a reporter aggressively, "One of these days I'm going to rip Woodeschick—and then he'll never get me out!" I guess this is the kind of thing Mauch was looking for, and I began thinking that I had been suppressed at first because I had just been brought along too fast by the White Sox.

This was true as far as baseball went because I did need the time to get used to big league pitching. The pitching at Indianapolis was tough enough, and it is difficult to even try to explain the superior quality of those that throw in the Bigs. But I was the same inside. Little things bothered me, like being the only big leaguer to ever come out of East Bakersfield and not being able to find a job there in off season. I even thought that if I'd grown up in Qualls things might have been different. In Qualls there was only a grocery store and a filling station, but my mother told me the wind blew it away.

Once I had achieved success, Dianne was after me all the time, too. She wanted me to become more forceful and outgoing. But I had always been an introvert—my brother, Pete, he's the extrovert, I'd tell Dianne. Pete, you can't mention anything he hasn't done and done better than the next guy. I could play better baseball but I doubted I could change my personality. I realized people were beginning to recognize me and that made me feel good. But I didn't want to be so well known that I couldn't go where I wanted, when I wanted. It even scared me, when I talked with people, how much they knew about me. Maybe this would be the year I could help the Phillies win the pennant, but that is where I wanted to leave it. Superstar or no superstar!

En route from Clearwater to Philadelphia I remembered what Paul Richards had once said about me: "If that young fella would stop thinking he ought to get a hit everytime he swings the bat, there is no telling how good he could be." Even during the past two seasons, which had been successes, I had fought myself at the plate instead of allowing my natural ability to take over. I would get upset real easy when I would hit the ball well and somebody would make a great play on me. But baseball always seemed to find a way to even up. In 1963 I had led the National League in assists for an outfielder with 25. However, Clemente won the Golden Glove award and this took the edge off of this accomplishment. I was still fighting myself, I guess, as I always found bad in something good.

Finally it was Tuesday, April 14, 1964, and the season was ready to start at home against the Mets in Connie Mack Stadium. It was time to play baseball and it was time to quit thinking so much. I had refused to sign my contract in January because I had expected more of a raise. I thought I was a better baseball player in 1963 than I was in 1962, even though the statistics didn't necessarily prove it. But I had gotten more big hits when they counted in 1963. I had also overcome my number one enemy—left-handed pitchers. In 1963 I had batted .295 against southpaws. I had borne down against them and even hit the untouchable Sandy Koufax for my share. The Phillies must have agreed with my way of thinking, or Gene Mauch convinced them what I should be paid, because my contract for 1964 jumped to $26,500 from 1963's $17,500, and that was an excellent raise in those days.

During the off season we had acquired ace pitcher Jim Bunning and catcher Gus Triandos from Detroit for Don Demeter and Jack Hamilton. I didn't know what to think of this trade when I first heard about it because Don Demeter was such a good ballplayer, but as it turned out it would be one of the best ones the Phillies ever made. Also, a kid named Richie Allen had made the club. He showed more power at the plate than I'd ever seen, but I couldn't figure what position he'd lock into. But on opening day the lineup card read:

Taylor	2b
Allen	3b
Gonzalez	cf
Callison	rf
Covington	lf
Sievers	1b
Dalrymple	c
Wine	ss

This lineup was promising and we swept the Mets on the fourteenth and fifteenth, with Tony Gonzalez hitting game winning three-run homers in each game. In the second game Jim Bunning picked up his first Phillie victory. On Thursday we headed for a five-game road trip—three in Chicago and two in New York. We came back to Connie Mack on the twenty-second, sporting a 6–1 record and finding ourselves in first place.

Fifteen thousand fans greeted us, and that following Friday against the Cubs, who we routed 10–0, I hit a two-run homer. Jim Bunning won number two, and in two games he had struck out 20 and only allowed a single run. We were off and running, and on April 29th we beat the Reds in Cincinnati 4–2 when I hit an RBI single in the seventh. Rookie Richie Allen, who was batting .442 at this point, had a home run, a triple, and two singles for the night. We were having fun!

On May 9th we blasted the Reds at Connie Mack. During that game Wes Covington became the first guy to ever hit a baseball to the far side of the giant clock atop the sixty-four-foot-high scoreboard in right center. He also had two singles and five RBIs as we won 11–3. I raised my average forty-two points to .250 by hitting two triples, a double, and a single.

The weeks moved swiftly, and on May 21st we worked over ace Juan Marichal and the Giants 7–2 at Candlestick. I went five for five, hitting a home run and batting in five runs. In the early part of the game Bobby Wine made a sensational play by taking a base hit away from one of the Giants, which would have put them ahead, and turned it into a twin killing. Everything was working for us! The standings after this game were:

Phillies	19–11
Giants	20–12
Cardinals	20–14

We were nearing the end of our second month and still in first place. It was hard to believe for us and the fans.

It was during this series with the Giants that I had borrowed Orlando Cepeda's forty-ounce bat. Wes Covington, when he saw me swinging it and I was complaining of a backache, said, "That's what happens when a little fella like you tries to swing a big man's bat." But that very day I went five for five, and how can anyone argue with that?

On June 14th we swept the Mets in a doubleheader at Connie Mack before 20,000 fans. I moved my average over .300 by doubling and homering in the nightcap. Richie Allen hit a home run that rocketed fifty feet higher than the scoreboard in right center. It hit the light tower. Historians would later recall that only Jimmy Foxx had ever cleared that right center-field fence and that was back in the twenties. Richie's ball must have traveled 500 feet before it hit the iron works. It was an opposite-field hit, to tell you how strong he was.

On June 21st we swept the Mets again for two in their new home in Queens, Shea Stadium. The two victories gave us a two-and-a-half-game lead. I was playing like I was one of the best players in the majors—maybe I was. This was our first look at Shea Stadium. I remember the lights being exceptional and it seemed like they turned night into day. I hit a two-run homer in the opener in the sixth inning.

More than forty-one thousand fans saw the games that day and it was a memorable occasion. In the first game, Jim Bunning pitched a perfect game. This was a hell of an experience. Nobody talked to Bunning, but the rest of us just hoped like hell nobody would hit us the ball. The pressure was incredible as none of us wanted to be responsible for an error or a cheap hit falling in our area. The other thing I remember was how poor the drainage system was there. It had rained before the game and the water in the outfield was shoe-top level. I had to change stockings three times. It was the wettest field I'd ever played on. In some places you couldn't even see the grass. Johnny Briggs, who was playing his first game for us while Bunning was pitching his no-hitter, said to me, "I was worried because I can't swim." In the second game I hit my eighth home run of the season into the second deck of seats near the right-field foul line. I never thought then how important the location of that shot would be when I'd be back in Shea sixteen days later. The standings after those games were:

Phillies	36–22
Giants	35–26

We had a two-and-one-half game lead and another month had almost passed, but we knew we had our work cut out for us. We left New York for Chicago. We played two there and moved on to a weekend series in St. Louis. We went from St. Louis to

Houston for two and then on to Los Angeles for a pair. We were losing our share of games on this tour, and when we arrived in San Francisco on July 3rd we found ourselves a game and a half behind the Giants.

We swept the Giants in the weekend series, putting us up a game and one-half. Not since the "Whiz Kids" of 1950 had the Phillies ever been in first place at the all-star break. The standings were: Phillies 47–28, Giants 47–31.

*   *   *

July 7, 1964
Shea Stadium
Queens, New York

Even though I was having a good season I hadn't expected to make the all-star team. I was a right fielder and so were Roberto Clemente and Hank Aaron. But in a surprise move, and no one was more surprised than me, Walter Alston selected me for the team. I was thrilled, of course, but didn't really expect I'd get a chance to play. But fate would lend a hand when Hank Aaron showed up at the park feeling ill. In the bottom of the fifth inning Alston sent me to the plate to pinch hit for teammate Jim Bunning. I popped out and thought that was that. But Alston kept me in the lineup by sending me out to right field. I wasn't out there long when Brooks Robinson ripped a gapper between Willie Mays and me. Willie dove and kept rolling one somersault after another as I retrieved the ball. When it was all over Brooks Robinson had a triple and the American League had tied the game at three. In the seventh the American League added another run and the score remained American League 4, National League 3 as we moved into the bottom of the ninth inning.

I didn't expect to bat in the bottom of the ninth inning as Dick Radatz was mowing everyone down. I'd faced him in the seventh and gotten ahold of a low fastball, driving it some 400 feet, where center fielder Mickey Mantle ran it down. It was just another long out. I hated those kind of outs!

As Willie Mays strolled to the plate I sat in the dugout just looking at all the people out there as the place was packed with some 50,000 fans. My eyes then focused on the mound at "The Monster," Dick Radatz. He'd been firing bullets and I just couldn't imagine anyone getting to him now. He had pitched to only six batters and struck out four. *If only I would have pulled my ball just a little*, I thought. It would have been a homer for sure if I'd pulled it just a hair.

Mays hadn't hit the ball out of the infield during his first three trips to the plate. In fact, Willie didn't even have his own Giants batting helmet with him. He was wearing one of the Braves hard hats. Quickly, Radatz had him down one ball and two strikes; but, then, for some reason, the Fiend tried to be careful, working the count to 3–2, and the next pitch was high, sending Willie to first base. Big Orlando Cepeda was next, but he was 0–20 in all-star competition and that could be good or bad. He was well overdue, but in these kind of games, no matter what one does during the regular season, he might never get a hit in an all-star game. I, and probably everyone else in the ballpark, was thinking, though, one swing and we win, as Cepeda had great power. Instead, when Orlando swung and missed strike two, Willie Mays broke for second and stole it clean.

Mays's presence at second base started to bother second baseman Bobby Richardson of the New York Yankees immediately. It would have been just like Willie to steal third, and he knew it. Consequently, Bobby kept bluffing toward second, and when Cepeda blooped a ball into short right field Richardson, out of position, couldn't get it, nor could Joe Pepitone, the first baseman. Mays raced to third while Pepitone picked up the ball, spun, and threw toward home. The ball took a high hop over catcher Elston Howard's raised glove, and Mays scored with the tying run as

Cepeda took second base. Speed merchant Curt Flood went in to run for Cepeda. Kenny Boyer of the St. Louis Cardinals was next to bat, and he had already homered earlier in the game. Boyer, trying to move Flood to third, fouled off a bunt attempt in his second strike and then popped up. This brought up Cincinnati Reds catcher Johnny Edwards. Johnny was intentionally walked to set up the double-play possibility. Alston told Hank Aaron to grab a bat to pinch hit for the Mets' Ron Hunt. Radatz had no trouble with Hank Aaron as he struck him out, and I was sorry to see that happen from the on-deck circle.

My mind kind of goes blank here as I walked to the plate. I only remember thinking, *Don't strike out!* The game was on the line. If we won, the National League would tie the series at seventeen games apiece. A series which was once ruled by the likes of Ruth, Gehrig, and Foxx. Now here I was! Johnny Callison from the streets of East Bakersfield. What the hell was I doing in this position with the eyes of the nation on me?

I kind of sneaked up to the plate, quietly reaching my bat across it to tap the other side one time. This procedure was kind of a ritual for me. I stepped back out of the box, for a second, to look at the giant who was only sixty feet six inches away. I didn't know a lot about Radatz other than they called him "The Monster" or "The Fiend of Fenway." Everyone had nicknames, but he looked like a monster to me. He stood six feet six inches and weighed at least 250 pounds. Yet, no matter how big, I determined, he still had to throw that ball by me—he hadn't done that yet. I had hit his pitch in the seventh inning, and I was digging in now as Radatz was glaring down trying to put the fear of God in me.

He reared and threw me a high hard one. I think I was determined to swing when he went into his motion, and I did! As soon as I swung, I thought it was a homer. You can just feel it—hear it! The line drive started as I finished my swing. I saw right fielder Rocky Colavito move three steps to his left, and then I watched the ball bounce off the orange beyond the auxiliary scoreboard. I was on cloud nine as I raced around the bases. By the time I'd rounded second I saw Radatz throw his glove into the dugout. Curt Flood, Johnny Edwards, and the rest of the National League all-stars mobbed me at home plate. It was a thrill, and I thought about the game being over, and a member of the Phillies had done the job.

I would hear afterwards that not since 1941, when Ted Williams poled a ninth-inning homer to win the game for the American League, had this particular classic game ever ended so dramatically. I remember thinking I was keeping pretty good company.

I've often thought about that day. I was named Most Valuable Player, and it is just something you never think would happen to you. Perhaps I was just destined to be there—I don't know what else would've made it happen. Ironically, Al Lopez of the White Sox was the manager of the American League players. He said, "I never thought of going to the mound to advise Radatz about Callison, because all I'd have told him was to fire it, and he did that."

Radatz said, "I thought I'd try something different, but it didn't work too good . . . as a rule, lefthanded batters are good low-ball hitters, and since I knew nothing about him, I pitched him low when he came up, in the seventh. He got pretty good wood on that one, so I decided to get the ball higher the second time."

As an afterthought, when we exited the National League dugout, Casey Stengel lingered to gaze longingly at the batting-order card which Alston had posted there. He must have reminisced about the great Yankee teams when he had won so many championships. Now he was the manager of the hapless New York Mets. "Leave it up, will ya?" he begged.

* * *

About the 1964 all-star game:

Pete Callison:
That was it! I couldn't have been prouder. People would stop

me on the street to say, "Aren't you Johnny Callison's brother?"

I'd say, "No, he's my brother. I was born first." But that was it—I mean, it was the whole deal!

Don Jones:

I'll never forget that day. I was sitting with a friend having a few beers and he called it. When Johnny came up in that clutch situation, he said, "He's going to hit one!" I didn't respond, but I kinda knew it, too, because Johnny always did things like that. I don't think my friend and I made a bet because it happened too fast. But we were both proud and it was a moment I'll never forget. I remember thinking at the time it was a difficult thing to believe that my boyhood friend was making such acclaim. But it didn't really surprise me—he simply had the talent from way back when I knew him as a kid.

Les Carpenter:

I think it was the first time they televised the all-star game by satellite. My wife and I were in Hawaii. We were walking in the airport to get our return trip back to California. By happenstance alone, we got in line behind movie actor John Wayne. When Johnny hit his home run we all saw it on screens that were displaying the game around the airport. My wife went crazy as she started shouting, "Les, that's our Johnny! John did it!"

Hearing the commotion behind him, the famous movie actor turned around to see what was going on. My wife was beside herself. "That's our Johnny! That's our Johnny," she kept repeating. "Mr. Wayne, the guy that just hit the home run to win the all-star game was our Johnny Callison!" John Wayne gave a hearty laugh and kissed my wife. We kidded her for some time thereafter, that she never took a bath for fear the kiss might rub off.

Dianne Callison:

I was with my mother and sister Bette. When Johnny hit that home run we were shocked. I started to cry and I just couldn't stop!

Lori Callison McGowan:

I was only six at the time but I knew something special had happened because reporters were around all the time. Dad brought us presents when he came back from New York, and that's about all I remember. But they took pictures of us all and I didn't really understand. Dad was just Dad to me, and I was always happy when he was home!

*   *   *

It was a time that stood out among others. I received telegrams and copies of newspaper clippings from all over the country. I even got a call from a "fag" suggesting I had a big "basket." This upset me so badly that when I got back to the room that night I looked in the mirror and thought someone was there. It was probably the most exciting time of my baseball career, but I was too caught up in the pennant race to fully appreciate it.

Pennant fever was raging in Philadelphia when we returned from a road trip on July 24th. More than five thousand fans mobbed us at Philadelphia International Airport, and I had a difficult time just making my way to our car. CALLISON FOR PRESIDENT placards charged. It was the first time I'd ever been considered for the White House, I thought, and I was feeling great!

On August 1st, before more than twenty-four thousand fans at Connie Mack, I helped Chris Short win another game by belting my eighteenth homer of the year. We won 6–1, maintaining a one-and-one-half-game lead over the Giants.

August 12th we routed the Chicago Cubs at Wrigley Field 13–5. The score was tied 5–5 when I came up in the sixth inning with the bases loaded. Left-hander Dick Ellsworth was on the mound and he had just beaned Tony Gonzalez. Johnny Briggs and Bobby Wine carried Tony off the field on a stretcher, and then Briggs went in to run for Gonzalez at first base.

Ellsworth must have been a little tenuous when I first came up. Most major league pitchers get upset when they hit an opponent in the head with a pitch. Anyway, Ellsworth's first pitch was a hanging curve ball, which I took for a called strike. I was really mad at myself when I let that one go by—it just hung there. But as I was cussing myself for taking that one, Ellsworth hung another. I took a cut at this one and deposited it in the right-field pavilion for my first National League grand slam home run. It was my nineteenth dinger of the year and my tenth off left-handed pitchers.

For some reason the mathematics interested the writers. They compared me to Billy Williams, who played for the Cubs and had already hit 25 home runs on the campaign—a left-hander who had hit only six of his home runs off of left-handed pitchers. They reported that Ruth, in 1927, had hit only nineteen home runs out of his sixty that year off lefties, and that nearly all of Roger Maris's 61 in 1961 had come off right-handers. Why, then, they asked, had I hit ten of nineteen off of portsiders?

I could never understand why people concerned themselves with these types of statistics. It was difficult enough to just get a hit in the Bigs, let alone worry about why you hit a left-hander or a right-hander the way that you did because of the side of the plate you swung from—but it mattered to them so I gave a response: "We were getting left-handers thrown at us every place we played. If you see enough of anything you're bound to catch up with it. Plus, those left-handers just keep hanging those curve balls!"

The "slam" in Chicago was a big thing for me and the club at the time. Probably a bigger personal hype was when I hit my first one during my rookie season in 1959 with the White Sox. I'll never forget that one as it was the only home run I hit that year. It was in Detroit, and right-hander Ray Narleski was pitching for the Tigers.

It was in the eighth inning when I came up, and I hit it off the right-field roof at Briggs Stadium.

About Tony Gonzalez: It was the fourth time Tony had been beaned this year. Al Jackson, Joe Gibbon, Bob Buhl, and now Ellsworth had hit him in the head. For some reason, and Tony couldn't explain it, he just froze at that last second before the ball would crash into his helmet. Ellsworth said, "He just doesn't move." Wes Covington commented, "I don't see how he gets hit, because nobody stands further away from the pate. He just freezes. He steps into the ball, and then seems unable to duck." As you know by now, I seldom made a comment, but I couldn't figure it out either. Tony was always a gamer, though. Cookie Rojas went with him to the hospital, and when Tony spoke he said, "I got a little hcadachc, got an aspirin?"

After this game Gene Mauch was quoted: "You get so you expect Callison to do things like that. As a matter of fact, I'm surprised when they get him out. I think he's a helluva hitter."

Mauch's comments were good to hear, but deep down I still didn't really believe in myself! I don't know why.

On August 15th we beat the Mets twice in a twilight doubleheader. It was our fourteenth win in sixteen meetings. Eighteen-year-old Rick (Ricky-Cool) Wise and Jim Bunning pitched great. I hit my twentieth home run over the right-field fence off lefty Al Jackson. Now, eleven of my twenty home runs were off left-handers. Richie Allen went six for nine in that doubleheader and was really contributing to our pennant chase. Once again we played in front of more than forty thousand fans in New York. The Mets didn't win many games but they had a helluva following.

On August twenty-third more than thirty-five thousand jam-packed Connie Mack Stadium to see us sweep the Pittsburgh Pirates in another pair. Mahaffey won the first game 2–0, with Frank Thomas hitting a two-run homer in the bottom of the ninth inning, sealing Art's two-hitter. In the nightcap it was 3–2 when I hit a two-RBI sacrifice fly. I had hit a solo home run (21st) which had tied the game earlier. But what I remember the most about this game was in the top of ninth inning. Smokey Burgess led off with a single. Gene Alley came in to run for him. He scored on Bill Mazeroski's double to right center—score 3–2. Ed Roebuck came in to relieve Rick Wise, who had pitched a great game. Jerry Lynch tagged one of his pitches to fairly deep right field. I gloved it and threw a one-bounce strike to third baseman Bobby Wine. Mazeroski had tagged up, and I wasn't sure I could get him and thought my throw was going to hit him in the back as I watched from the outfield. Bobby put the tag on him and it was a thrill for me. Virdon singled, but then Roebuck struck out Bob Bailey to end the game. With this victory we took a seven-and-one-half game lead. I felt pretty good because I'd driven in all the runs and, more importantly, I'd made the big defensive play to save the game. At this point, I couldn't see anything but the world championship for the Phillies.

We were riding high into the crunch month of September, and on the first day of this month we were matched at Connie Mack Stadium with the Houston Colt 45's. Jim Bunning and Skinny Brown were locked in a scoreless tie in the 7th inning. Skinny Brown was throwing his knuckleballs, and none of us could catch up with them. However, in the seventh inning I hit one of his best in the seats for a home run to break the tie. Wes Covington hit the next knuckler out. Our next hitter was Frank Thomas. Frank hit a slider for another home run. Richie Allen hit an inside-the-park home run in the eighth, and that was enough for Jim Bunning to secure his sixth straight victory and fifteenth on the campaign, even if he yielded a three-run homer to Joe Gaines in the ninth before wrapping it up. The victory put us five and one-half games in front of the Reds (the Giants were fading). Allen's ball was timely and a terrific smash which bounced about a foot in front of the center-field flagpole (445 feet). It would have been a triple, but Carroll Hardy, the Colt 45's center fielder, started to make his throw and held back. George Myatt, third base coach, waved him all the way, and Allen turned on his speed, too, for his twenty-fifth home run.

My home run that night was my twenty-fourth.

On September 5th we put the Giants away for good when, after trailing 3–1, Frank Thomas hit a two-run homer to tie the game in the eighth inning. For some crazy reason Mauch had me batting in the seventh position this game, and as luck would have it I came up after Gus Triandos doubled. In this same inning, I hit a game-winning single, driving in Gus, and we thought Mauch was a genius and nothing could stop us now.

The season moved to mid-September, and we closed out our road trip by beating Houston 4–1. I hit a single, a double, and a two-run homer (number 27), which gave us a six-and-one-half-game lead with only fourteen games left to play. Our magic number was thirteen, and we were on our way back to Philadelphia for a long home stand to wrap it up as the standings read convincingly in our favor:

Phillies	87–57
Cardinals	80–63
Giants	80–65
Redlegs	79–64

*   *   *

Dianne Callison:

The season had been full. Johnny's mom and dad even visited us for the first time in Philadelphia during the week of Mother's Day. On May 10th we were playing Cincinnati at home and Johnny's parents sat in the box seat behind home plate with me. Johnny's mom had a corsage of tiny roses pinned to her print dress and sat there with a transistor radio plug in her left ear. She couldn't have been prouder, and we were happy to have them there.

During the game she told me a story I hadn't heard before, but it was so typically Johnny. She said, "When he was a youngster

115

he'd come home after a game, and if I didn't ask him how he did, he would never say. Once, in a county all-star game he hit a home run over the scoreboard, but I had to hear about it from someone else."

Johnny would've loved to have had a big day that day when his folks were there, but such things never really work out. The Reds beat us 2–0 and he went hitless. He didn't even have tough chances in the field. After the game, when he walked out of the clubhouse where we were waiting for him, he grimaced, smiled, shrugged his shoulders, and nobody could really think of anything to say. So, we all went to dinner at Old Original Bookbinder's. The following Tuesday we helped his parents celebrate their thirty-third wedding anniversary, and during that time Johnny's mom said, "Johnny has always been truthful. He's always been like that. I don't think the publicity he got affected him. He's not the type of person to be swayed, one way or the other. He's always been calm."

Reporters would talk to me, asking me why he wouldn't talk more, or pat himself on the back. They'd tell me when he's in a good streak Johnny will just look at his shoes and say, "I'm seeing the ball good. When I'm seeing the ball good, I'm gonna hit it. I could make up a bunch of stuff about changing my stance and all that, like some other guys, but it's not true. I'm just seeing the ball good. As for popping off, I'm never going to pop off. There are a lot of things I don't know about the game. If I keep quiet, then nobody else will know. If I pop off, then everybody will know. It just seems like every time I've made a statement in the past, I've stuck my foot in my mouth."

I guess he might have frustrated some of the writers but not me. I never really tried to change him. He never brought the game home with him. He might walk in and say he had a lousy day, but that was the end of it. The things that bother him he keeps to himself, and I know that is not really good for him but I don't think he would have ever changed. Frankly, I'm just as happy he was that way rather than coming home and kicking a door down.

On July 29th, Johnny was honored by the Bakersfield JBA. Their annual all-star game was dedicated to him. The trophy bore the inscription OUR OWN ALL-STAR, JOHNNY CALLISON, CONGRATULATIONS, BAKERSFIELD JBA AND KERN KIWANIS, JULY 29, 1964. Since Johnny couldn't be there, his parents accepted the award from Coach Les Carpenter at Sam Lynn Park that night.

Now we were ready to move into the home stretch of the season. In August we received word that the city of Bakersfield had proclaimed Sunday, September 20th, as Johnny Callison Day, and a ceremony would be held at the game between the Phillies and the Dodgers on that date. The team left Houston on September 16th for a four-game series with the Dodgers, who were prepared to decrease that magic number from thirteen.

When the day came, a large contingent of Bakersfield boosters and the entire Exchange Club were present. Johnny's family and many of our friends were at the Chavez Ravine for the ceremony, held just before the game. Johnny was met at home plate by the delegation, who presented the official key to the City of Bakersfield. He was given a proclamation by the mayor that read:

WHEREAS, Baseball is recognized as the Number One sport in the world, enjoyed by the entire family, and

WHEREAS, JOHNNY CALLISON has reached the pinnacle in the baseball world by his association with the Philadelphia Phillies and through individual and team efforts has enriched the game of baseball and is a living symbol of what may be accomplished by youth and is an inspiration to those young Little Leaguers throughout the world, and

WHEREAS, he has spread the name and fame of BAKERSFIELD throughout the world, and

WHEREAS, the City of Bakersfield is highly honored to call him a native son, and

WHEREAS, the Bakersfield Exchange Club will salute him Sunday, September 20, 1964, at Chavez Ravine in a baseball testimonial,

117

NOW, THEREFORE, I, GENE WINER, MAYOR of the City of Bakersfield, do hereby proudly proclaim the day, Sunday, September 20, 1964, as "JOHNNY CALLISON DAY" in Bakersfield.

DATED at Bakersfield, California, this 19th day of August, 1964.

*　　*　　*

Twenty-five years have passed and it just won't go away. After my big day in L.A. we came back to Philadelphia for a seven-game home stand. After that we had three on the road against St. Louis and two at Cincinnati. We had a six-and-one-half-game lead, and what could look better? To simplify what such a lead means with twelve games left, I'll try to explain. If we would have won six of twelve, we'd have it. If one of the contenders would lose six of twelve, we'd have it. What happened was against all probabilities—we didn't win and they didn't lose!

It all started on Monday, September 21st. The Cincinnati Reds came to Connie Mack. More than 20,000 were in the stands and they were feeling pretty confident, as were we. The score was 0–0 in the sixth inning and Frank Robinson was at bat, with Chico Ruiz edging off third base. Who cared? I guess the Reds did, because they were still in the race, and that's what makes this play so unbelievable. Man on third, game tied, Reds in the race, and their big man, Frank Robinson, at the plate. Suddenly, with no instruction to do so, Chico broke for home. Mahaffey, in the middle of his wind-up, picked up the blur in his peripheral vision for a split second. Art hurried through the final movements of his delivery and sailed an errant pitch to the right of catcher Clay Dalrymple. Ruiz came in standing up with a big smile on his face. It would be the game's only run. Dick Sisler, the Reds' manager, said after the game, "If I'd had a gun, I would have shot him."

The next night Chris Short, who had 17 wins, was routed 9–2. On the 23rd, Dennis Bennett, whose arm was racked with tendonitis, lasted six innings, but we lost 6–4. The Reds swept us and the Milwaukee Braves were next.

Jim Bunning worked the first game against the Braves and we could do nothing. He pitched six innings and we calmly lost it 5–3. We had lost four in a row, but we were still in control and were determined to get our act together the next night. Our determination made the game last twelve innings, but we lost it 7–5, with Chris Short taking the loss. We were leading 1–0 going into the top of the seventh, but Dalrymple tipped Dennis Menke's bat with his glove for a catcher's interference call, and it set up a two-run Braves rally. Then when we were trailing 3–1 in the eighth, I tied the score with a two-run homer. The Braves got two in the top of the tenth, but Richie Allen hit an inside-the-park homer to tie the score again. However, Frank Thomas, who had removed the cast from his thumb himself, so that he could play, was hit a potential double-play ball. It bounced off his rusty glove, and the Braves went on to win 7–5.

On September 26th we carried a 4–3 lead into the ninth, only to lose 6–4, with Mahaffey being the victim after Bobby Shantz, who had come in the eighth inning to relieve, yielded a three-run triple to Rico Carty, giving the Braves a 6–4 win.

We had lost six in a row at home now and were tied with the Reds for first place. The most difficult thing to believe was that the Reds had won eight straight games while we lost six. The Philadelphia boo-birds returned to greet us for our final game against the Braves.

Jim Bunning made the start again and blew a 3–2 lead, lasting only three innings. I hit three home runs trying to salvage this one, but we lost 14–8, and for the first time since July 16th we were out of first place, one game behind Cincinnati, who had won their ninth straight. After the game Mauch refused to allow reporters in the clubhouse and just paced around chain-smoking. I think we were all waiting for him to become outrageous. Perhaps, if he would've, it might have changed things. He had always been such a tyrant, but now he seemed to prefer being a recluse.

When I met Dianne at the car she was all smiles, saying, "You hit three home runs—one was your hundredth!"

I could only respond, "But we lost!"

And all of us players were glad to be getting out of Connie Mack—we had lost seven straight and were headed for St. Louis, which was trailing by only a half game.

We moved to St. Louis and lost 5–1 (Short), 4–2 (Bennett), and 8–5 (Bunning). In one of those games I was so sick I was white. Late in the game Mauch asked me to pinch hit and I couldn't believe it. I hit a single, and when I reached first base I called for a jacket because I had the chills so badly. When I got the coat I was too weak to button it up. It seemed like an omen when Bill White, the Cardinal first baseman, reached over and buttoned it up for me.

When we left St. Louis we were two and one-half games behind the Cardinals, and we only had two to play. Short and Bunning beat Cincinnati in the last two games, but the Cardinals won one of three to win the pennant on the last day of the season. After 162 games it was finally over. If somewhere along the line we had just won one more game it wouldn't have been, and that was the hardest pill to swallow.

Why? This word will always haunt us—those that played then. Was it Mauch's fault not resting Bunning and Short? Why didn't he give Ray Culp a shot? Were we overachievers? I prefer to leave it with a question. How could we lose all those games and how could St. Louis win all those games? The 1969 Mets won the World Series, the 1987 Twins won the World Series. Why? There are no answers. Sometimes things just happen that way!

When we flew back from Cincinnati, on October 4th, we didn't know what to expect—maybe a lynching. It has been said Philadelphia fans are better losers than winners. They were that night, as signs saluted us rather than burying us. Gene Mauch insisted on being the first one off the plane, and he handled it well. We were all shell-shocked and felt as sorry for the fans as we did for ourselves. What followed was even worse as, for some reason, the city of Philadelphia got tabbed as being losers for what we had failed to do, and I could never figure that one out.

My final thoughts on the 1964 season are that for 150 games we played well. We were loose and just didn't make mistakes. In those last 12 games we made errors, didn't hit as a team, and our pitching completely failed us. For example, in 4 games against the Braves they pounded our pitchers for thirty-two runs and an incredible fifty-nine hits. Twenty-two of those hits came in the 14–8 loss when I hit three home runs. The booing didn't help either. It was the worst I'd ever heard. How anyone could boo a Richie Allen, after the season he had as a rookie, I will never be able to understand. The fans' negative reaction made us all tense and irritable!

*   *   *

John Sletten:

I'll never forget it! I was a sophomore in college at the time and in the midst of a football campaign. I'd been following the Phillies' plight via the newspaper, of course, and was rooting for them like most other people in the country. I just kept waiting for them to win or for St. Louis or Cincinnati to lose, but it didn't happen.

On game day, in college football, one is consumed nearly the entire day. Game breakfast, game chapel service, going to the field, taping, chalk talk, pregame practice, the game itself, and the aftermath. I remember on the morning of September the 26th being consumed with the National League pennant race. The Phillies had lost five straight games and their lead had dwindled from six and one-half to one. At breakfast, I had my face buried in the newspaper. A teammate or two asked, "What's so interesting?" Thinking, I'm sure, that I was reading about our upcoming game. I told them I was reading about the Phillies.

Most of the players that played on my team at that time were from Minnesota and couldn't have cared less about what was happening in Philadelphia. So, you can imagine the lack of response. But my mind was with the Phillies that day, and all during our game I kept wondering if they were winning, whether I was on the football field or not. I was shocked when I found out after our game that they had lost again.

When the Phillies lost the following Sunday, Monday, Tuesday, and Wednesday I was distraught, and I felt sure they would lose it all. And they did! The St. Louis Cardinals had stolen the pennant from the Phillies by sneaking in through the back door. I don't know why the Phillies' blowing the pennant, this particular year, bothered me so immensely. As I said before, I was an avid baseball fan. Maybe it was because my Phillies (in my fantasy major leagues) always won the pennant. At any rate, I had to research what had happened.

It had been written that the city of Philadelphia loves a loser. When the new, young 1964 Phillies seemed to have winning ways, the city's inhabitants didn't know what to do—laugh or cry. There is no town anywhere that scorns a winner and loves a loser quite like the City of Brotherly Love. During this year the city of Philadelphia was torn. It was in danger of having a winner in the Phillies, many of the players being the same forlorn fellas who set a National League record in 1961 of losing twenty-three straight games. This was a great time for the real Philly fan. There was one lunatic who hid out in the left-field bleachers at archaic Connie Mack Stadium and started whipping firecrackers at the hometown outfielders. Hot dog wrappers began filtering down from the stands, causing pitchers and infielders to step in pools of ketchup, mustard, and waxed paper. Most of the Philadelphia Phillies fans suddenly became experts about the Phillies, and everyone believed they, alone, could spot their shortcomings.

But the dreams began during the 1962 season when the Phillies became the hottest team in baseball by winning thirty of

122

their last forty-four games. The team had picked up twenty-six more wins in one season and played .500 baseball for the first time in nine years. When the 1963 season began, no one believed the Phillies would ever lose twenty-three straight games again. Woe to the true grit of the Phillies fans. Suddenly, they had .300 hitters in Johnny Callison, Don Demeter, and Tony Gonzalez. The Phillies had become real. Before the 1964 season they had given up a .300 hitter for a quality pitcher in Jim Bunning. Now with hitting and pitching (Bunning, Short, Mahaffey), they could enter a campaign with certain confidence that they could win their share. Phillies fans—they didn't know quite what to do. What they did was root, root, root for the home team and enjoyed their Phillies' first-place standings right up till the end. When the team didn't quite make it, they didn't become angry. It was more like the prodigal sons had returned home. The fans were safe! Placards greeted the Phillies home, displaying the words "Welcome Phillies—You played like the Champs you'll be in '65." What a relief. Next year they could boo them on to victory again!

*　　*　　*

I'll never forget that night in St. Louis. There were two teams in first place in the National League, and we were neither of them. It was so sad, so very terribly sad, and I was lying face down on a table in the clubhouse with a virus. I hadn't been able to hold food all day. My head throbbed and I had a bad cold. My body was chilled, my cheeks were sunken when I looked in the mirror. I was waiting for the doctor, and when he arrived, he told me to go back to the hotel to get in bed. Gene Mauch protested. I stayed.

Dennis Bennett was on the mound, and he had taken pills for the pain he knew would wrack his shoulder as soon as he began to warm up. The Cardinals got to him for three runs but he still continued. Sure enough, a messenger came into the clubhouse in the fifth inning wanting to know if I could muster up enough strength for one at bat. My head felt so light when I walked to the plate I thought I'd fly up like a balloon. I hit a single, and as I stood at first base, after Bill White (Cardinals' first baseman) helped me button my jacket, I thought: *Where did it all go—the magic of the season.* And it went so fast!

Less than two weeks before, we'd led the league by six and one-half. Things looked great, but I was cautiously suspicious and I thought the team was too relaxed. Some of the players were already spending their World Series money. I threw caution to the wind when I told some of them that I didn't want to hear about the numbers. When we clinch it I'll be convinced. I told them if we lost so many in a row, and they win so many in a row, we'll be right back where we started. I just had this bad feeling, but even I didn't believe what eventually transpired.

Not that I was smarter than anyone else; I'd just played on losing teams all of my life. I played on one of the worst teams ever in the minors. I'd never played with a winner until I joined the White Sox in 1959. And the only way I knew how to win was to bear down all the time. I didn't see the team ready to bear down when we left Houston to make our final home stand to clinch the pennant.

I guess I'd become a team leader. I felt it was my duty to tell them I didn't think we had it won until we'd clinched it. Inside, I felt as though some of the guys were putting more pressure on me to hold up my end. I did, but one man is not a team! If there was any consolation in this bitter turn of events it was that I'd given everything I could give and more.

"We still love you!" shouted more than 12,000 people at Philadelphia International Airport when we arrived home from Cincinnati. I thought back to that late night in July when they wanted me for president—it was a much sweeter tune. "We'll get 'em next year, Johnny. We love you, Cookie, and you're still our boy, Richie." Their cries echoed into the night. Horns honked, bells clanged, and poetic pennants fluttered in the dismal evening breeze. If there is anything a ballplayer hates to hear uttered, it's "Wait 'til next year!" Especially when it should have been this year and you're emotionally and physically spent.

Gene Mauch was a class act. He was first off the ramp and first said, "This [pennant race] was the only thing I ever went after in my life that I felt I had a chance at and didn't win. This [the fans' reception] makes me feel like we should have won—won it for the fans." Mauch looked at the placards saying "We Still Love You!" He said, "Let's get that 'still' out of there."

So, it was finally over and we, the players, had to live with it. It was just a damn shame. We had battled so hard all year and I didn't remember an easy series. They all threw the best pitchers at us. Then, at the end, this lousy thing happens. The long summer's effort had reduced me from 189 pounds to 161. There seemed nothing left of me but sinew, bone, and a sad, painful anger which was festering in me like it never had before or since. It seemed like I'd always just missed! *Why? Why?* I just kept asking myself.

The Cardinals even felt sorry for us. Dick Groat, the Redbirds' great shortstop, said, "If they rap Mauch for fouling up his pitching, or anything else, they're stupid. Nobody managed like he did this year. When we went out against a Mauch team, we knew he's gonna play it to the hilt. Without Mauch, the Phils would never get this far."

I'll never forget Gene, sitting in front of a locker after the news came in on the radio that St. Louis had beaten the Mets to win the pennant. The place had become littered with telegrams from Philadelphians. "Read 'em for yourself." Mauch shrugged. "Most of them say it's been a tremendous season anyway, and I guess it has. Aw, we're old news now. But maybe tomorrow we'll be new news."

There was an eerie silence in the clubhouse, broken only when someone threw a beer can across the room in disgust. About that time Richie Allen chimed in, "I never thought we had it won, even when the magic number was seven. The kinds of games we won all year, people started winning from us. Ever since that guy stole home to beat us, twelve, thirteen games ago, the black cat's been on us."

Mayo Smith, former Phillie manager said, "If I hadn't seen it, I wouldn't believe it. No club in history ever got so many bad breaks with a pennant in its hands. You'll never see this again."

I say, "Who wants to?"

*　　*　　*

John Sletten:

The Cardinals beat the Yankees in the World Series in seven games. After the series Yogi Berra was fired as Yankee manager because of his alleged lack of control and communication with his players. Johnny Keane, Cardinal manager, resigned and was hired by the Yankees as manager for the 1965 season.

Back in Minnesota, at college, I was furious when Ken Boyer was named the National League's most valuable player. It was a joke, as it often is, because the award, for some reason, goes to the pennant winner. No one, in my opinion has ever been a more valuable player than Johnny Callison was to the 1964 Phillies. But it doesn't work that way.

I would never take anything away from Kenny Boyer because he was always one of my boyhood heroes. It was just that Johnny Callison was more valuable to his club. Even Boyer was shocked when he was notified of the award! Forgetting about the fact that Callison had played in 162 games, scored 101 runs, 179 hits, 30 doubles, 10 triples, 31 home runs, 104 RBIs, and batted for an average of .274 and slugged for .492. For the third straight season he'd led the National League in assists, getting credit for 19 this year. He was also the "Clutch King" of the majors by winning games with 5 home runs, 6 other hits, and 1 sacrifice fly. Kenny Boyer finished tenth in this category.

To compare: Boyer played in 162 games, scored 100 runs,

collected 185 hits, 30 doubles, 10 triples, 24 home runs, and batted in 119. He hit .295 and slugged for an average of .489. The statistics are close, granted, but who was more valuable? The Cardinals won the pennant and Johnny Callison just missed one more time.

*   *   *

No matter how bad it turned out, it was a helluva year. Times like 1964 will never return, and I was glad to be part of it. Back then, a Phillies scorecard was $.15, which included a free pencil. A box seat $3.25, reserved seat $2.25, general attendance $1.50, and a bleacher seat $.75. Ortlieb was Philadelphia's greatest beer of all, with the zip-top can.

There was a new hit record with a rock-and-roll rhythm called "Go-Go Phillies of '64" by the Umpires. This particular tune, of course, was endorsed by "Rifle Arm" Johnny Callison, "Top Reliever" Jack Baldschun, and "Speed Merchant" Tony Taylor.

For the players, Shapiro Shoes granted any player hitting his first home run in Connie Mack stadium a pair of shoes for each member of a player's family. Any pitcher pitching his first shutout received the same benefit.

It was a time when Budget Rent-a-Car would give you wheels for $5.00 per day plus 5 cents a mile. What more could a guy want?

And for the fans, Concession prices were:

Coca-Cola	$.15
Beer	.40
Hoagie	.50
Cracker Jack	.25
Cigarettes	.40

*   *   *

On October the 8th, I received a letter from James H. J. Tate, mayor of Philadelphia:

Dear John:

On behalf of the people of Philadelphia, I want to congratulate you and your teammates for the wonderful job you did this season.

You were truly the "Fighting Phillies" as you provided thrill after thrill for Philadelphians of all ages. There always was action-packed excitement whenever the team took the field.

Even though disappointment has mixed in with the happy events of the season, I want you to know that you have thousands of loyal followers, including myself, who look to 1965 with great enthusiasm and anticipation. I am sure you know you can count on our support.

Your play this season was particularly outstanding. You have become the idol of just about every Philadelphia baseball fan, young and old alike. We are hopeful that you will have many more successful seasons.

We hope that you enjoy a restful winter and be in perfect condition when spring training camp begins next February.

With all good wishes and kindest personal regards, I am

Sincerely yours,
James H.J. Tate, Mayor

*　　*　　*

A fitting conclusion to the year 1964 came in a Christmas card. "Seasons Greetings" was scrolled on its front. Inside the message read:

'Twas the night before the Series
when all through the park
Not a creature was stirring
not even a lark
Our tickets were packed with
loving care
In fond hopes that customers
would soon be there.
The players were nestled all snug
in their beds
While visions of home runs danced
in their heads
When out on the field there arose
such a clatter
They sprang from their beds to see
what was the matter
Away to the window they flew like
a flash
Tore open the shutters and threw
up the sash
The moon on the breast of the new
painted seats
Gave a luster of game time to
objects below
When, what to their wondering eyes
should appear
But the Saint Louis Cardinals and
all of their gear
More rapid than Eagles the Cardinals
came
Whistled at, cheered and called by name
As the scene was shuttered out and
the sash drawn down
The trundle back to bed was not a
path to dread

But a path rather, leading to victory
in the year ahead.
We wish you the Very Merriest of
Christmases and the Happiest New Year

signed by: Joe Scott

"Okies": Back row, brother Pete and sister Joy Lu; Front row, me, Mom, and sister Judy Ann

First spring training with White Sox, 1958

Mom and I, Mother's Day
at Connie Mack Stadium,
May 10, 1964

Dad and I, Mother's Day
at Connie Mack Stadium,
May 10, 1964

A home run at Connie Mack in 1964 for number 6. Dick Allen (15) scored in front of me

There's no better feeling than getting ahold of a fastball. Richie Allen waits with a "low five" (1964)

1964 and I had it all—except the fur, Dianne recalls

The clip from the *New York Times* that is displayed in the Baseball Hall of Fame in the All Star game section at Cooperstown, New York

Crossing home plate after hitting game winning homer in the 1964 All Star game. There to greet me: Walter Alston, Johnny Edwards, Kenny Boyer, Dick Groat, Willie Mays, Roberto Clemente, Juan Marichal, and the rest of the National League All Stars

1964 baseball card

Callison's 3-Run HR With Two Out in 9th Gives NL 7-4 Victory

Stars of the 1964 All Star game: Willie Mays Juan Marichal and me

The President of the National League, Warren Giles, congratulates me after All Star game-winning homer in 1964

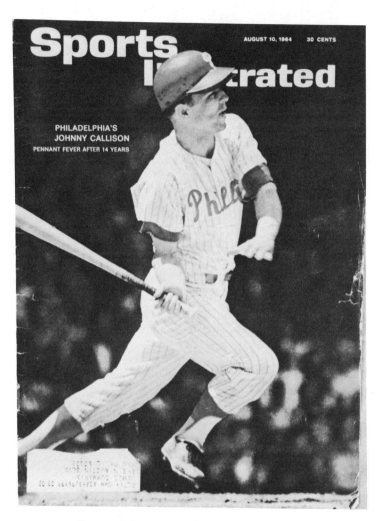

Cover of *Sports Illustrated*, August 1964

A Basebowl: Me and the "Duke of Flatbush,"
Duke Snider, Spring of 1964

The "Boys of Summer" 1964. In a game against the Houston Colt 45s, I hit a homer off knuckleball pitcher Skinny Brown. Wes Covington hit the next knuckler out. Frank Thomas hit a slider out. And finished off a string of four consecutive homers in one inning with an inside-the-park home run. A rare shot of Allen and Thomas together (remember that little confrontation I stirred up between the two).

My three girls (clockwise from top): Lauri, Cindy and Sherri

With Dianne in 1990

In some good company in 1983

On the one hundredth anniversary of the Phillies (1983) I was voted by the fans as one of the greats.

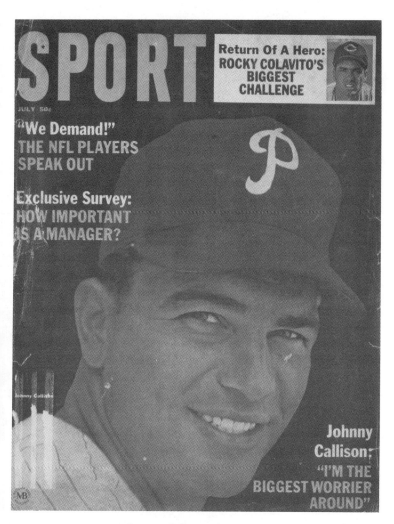

Cover of *Sport*, July 1964

For Mrs. Hammitt: At last
a Cub, 1970

In the end a Yankee, 1972

Chapter Six

Seasons in the Sun

Gatsby believed in the green light, the orgiastic future that year by year recedes before us. It eluded us then, but that's no matter—tomorrow we will run faster, stretch out our arms farther. . . . And one fine morning—
So we beat on, boats against the current, borne back ceaselessly into the past.

—F. Scott Fitzgerald, *The Great Gatsby*

Everyone I've met for the past twenty-five years has asked me what happened to the Phillies in 1965. We were a team that had been built and molded by an ingenious manager, Gene Mauch, from 1960 through the grand season of 1964. Wes just missed that year, and everyone thought we'd just be that much better in 1965. Maybe not that much better, but certainly more seasoned, and this seasoning would assure us of a pennant. We were young and had performed above all expectations in 1964. Why not? Why shouldn't we have done better in 1965?

Ironically, 1965 was my most productive season statistically, and my salary had increased from $17,500 in 1963 to $26,400 in 1964 to $45,000 in 1965. Willie Mays signed for $105,000 in 1965 when, at the same time, my manager Gene Mauch was being quoted as saying I was the most complete player to come into the league since Willie—hitting, running, throwing and going after a ball. Hearing all this rhetoric, I was convinced great financial rewards were on the close horizons. I remember being pumped at the time.

During the off season Mauch added three key players to try and insure our winning the National League pennant. We needed a right-handed power hitter and we got one. Dick Stuart, a terrific hitter, seemed to be the man. There was one problem with Stuart, however—he couldn't field a lick. Before the season started, it was written he should provide the greatest power and possibly the worst fielding at first base in the history of the Phillies. Stuart was coming over from the American League, where, during the past two seasons, he amassed 75 homers and 232 runs batted in. It was thought the left-field stands in Connie Mack Stadium would be an inviting target for this long-ball hitter. At first, this seemed great to me because I welcomed another right-handed power hitter to go along with Dick Allen. Maybe, now, we'd see more right-handed pitchers.

Additionally, we added left-handed and controversial Bo Belinsky to the staff. We traded away our sore-armed left-hander Dennis Bennent for righty Ray Herbert.

On paper the team appeared to have improved greatly, and even Gene Mauch described our club as the best team he might ever manage. We did seem set! We had Bunning and Short returning off great seasons. The addition of Belinsky and Herbert seemed to give us a good rotation, especially if Mahaffey and Culp came into play positively. If all remained healthy, we had six excellent starters which the lack thereof doomed us at the end of the 1964 campaign. Our infield seemed set with Stuart at first (in the late innings we could substitute him for defense), Taylor sound at second. Allen at third (his defense seemed improved from making the most errors in the National League the year before), and we had a good situation at short with Amaro, Wine, and Rojas capable of playing there with equal talents. Catching was good. Dalrymple came in much better shape, having lost fifteen pounds, and we had Triandos and rookie Pat Corrales to back him up. The outfield was set with

Gonzalez, Briggs, Rojas, Covington, and, of course, old number 6.

Even the bullpen looked strong with Baldschun and Roebuck. I couldn't see what could go wrong, but it did. In 1964 there was that special chemistry between us. Everybody rooted for the other guy. There was no set lineup except for Dick Allen and myself. The addition of "Dr. Strange-glove" (Dick Stuart) and Bo Belinsky didn't help our mix. Dick Allen, our sensational rookie, had his share of controversy the year before, and when Stuart and Belinsky arrived, they had been known to hit the headlines for more than winning games as well. As the season began we were expected to soar, and perhaps that put more pressure on us as well. Also, every team in the league was looking at us. We were now a team to beat!

It was the mid-sixties, and times in the world were changing rapidly around us also, as well as in baseball. Before the baseball season even began, such great people as Sir Winston Churchill, T. S. Eliot, and Nat King Cole had passed during the winter of this year. President Lyndon Johnson was inaugurated for his first and only elected term, and in March Martin Luther King made his famous freedom march on Selma, Alabama. The children were now seen on skateboards, and American planes were dropping napalm bombs on Vietnam.

In baseball, the directors of the Milwaukee Braves requested permission from the league to move to Atlanta, Georgia, for the 1965 season. However, the league ruled that due to the year remaining on the Milwaukee stadium lease and due to threatened litigation on the part of the city of Milwaukee, the Braves were required to remain in Milwaukee for 1965 but could move south in 1966. I'll never forget some of those games in Milwaukee that year when the crowd was under one thousand. Also, a baseball institution, the "Old Professor," Casey Stengel, was forced to retire. He had broken a hip on New Year's Eve and this injury forced him out during midseason. He retired from a long managerial career which included ten pennants with the Yankees and three and one-half years of fun with the New York Mets.

A big thing happened this year when the first free-agent draft was instituted to help equalize the distribution of talent and to cut down on large bonus outlays to untried green talent. A new commissioner was named in General William Eckert, a man who soon became known for his lack of public presence, and the Houston Astrodome had opened in the spring—baseball's first enclosed, air-conditioned stadium. The park was billed as the Eighth Wonder of the World, and its billing was at least enough of a conversation piece to triple Houston's attendance to more than two million. Additionally, the Colt 45's became nicknamed the Astros.

We were the first team to play a regular season game against the Astros in the Astrodome. It was our season opener on Tuesday, April 13, 1965. We won 2–0 as Chris Short struck out eleven, with Dick Allen hitting a two-run homer for the winning runs. Ruben Amaro opened the third inning with a line-drive single to left, and Short, called on to sacrifice, did it perfectly. Then, Tony Taylor dribbled one to the mound for the second out—the rally seemed about to die. Dick Allen strolled to the plate. He settled in the batter's box and fouled off pitcher Bob Bruce's first pitch. He took two balls and ripped the next pitch. From the crack of the bat I knew it was a goner. He hit it very well toward the deepest part of the air-conditioned stadium. Obviously, there was no wind to help or hinder the ball. It was a true shot which landed in the center-field seats, a few feet to the right of dead center. It was funny; the Astro fans cheered politely as Allen circled the bases behind Amaro, but I was more enthusiastic when I greeted him at home plate. It was the first home run ever hit at the Astrodome in a regular-season game. And as time passed, it would prove to be one of the most difficult places to ever hit a home run.

We didn't have that bad a year in 1965. We won 85 games and lost 76, but we finished in sixth place, to show how keen the competition was. I played in 159 games, batting .262, hitting my career high of 32 home runs with 101 runs batted in. I scored 93 runs and had a slugging percentage of .509. I led the league with 16 triples and hit 25 doubles. Dick Allen batted .302, had 20 home runs, and batted in 85. However, our new acquisitions failed to perform. Dick Stuart played in 144 games, batting a lowly .234, although he did hit 28 homers and knocked in 95 runs. Bunning won 19, Short won 18, and Culp won 14. Belinsky won 4 and lost 9, and Ray Herbert won 5 and lost 8. The trades just didn't work and neither did we as a team.

I do remember a few highlights, however. On June 6, 1965, I hit three homers against the Cubs in a doubleheader. We won both games, and I saved the first game for Ray Culp's five-hitter by making a great catch in right field. In the second game I hit a home run in the first inning off Larry Jackson and one in the third inning off Larry, breaking my bat. Everyone was saying at the time that they'd never seen someone hit a home run before while breaking a bat. I hit my third home run off Ernie Broglio in the ninth inning— that one was a goner! It was the second time I'd hit three homers in one game. My first was just the year before against the Braves in September of 1964 during our fatal stretch run. One of those shots was the 100th of my career.

Also, I was named to the National League all-star team for the third time. Gene Mauch was the manager of the National League all stars and selected Cookie Rojas and me for the game as alternates. The game was played in Minneapolis, Minnesota, on July 8th, but neither Cookie nor I got into the game. Oh, what a difference a year makes!

For some reason we just couldn't get it all going in 1965. Mauch became irritable, and I began feeling everything was my fault, even though I was having my best year. But I never worked harder, even though Gene didn't think so as he thought I should be shagging more fly balls in the outfield before games. I explained that it just tired me out more. On the other hand, I took batting practice until my hands blistered. That particular year I seemed to put myself under tremendous emotional strain.

Even though I was knocking more homers and runs in than I ever had, I couldn't keep my average where I wanted it or thought it should be. Sometimes I'd go home from the ballpark and just black out from battling myself, the bat, the pitchers, Gene, and everything. When I was hitting, everything I did looked good to people. When I was going bad, I fought myself the hardest. To Mauch and others it may have seemed that I wasn't trying, but that's when I was trying the most. Mauch didn't agree, and that's when our troubles began in Philadelphia. To this day, I don't care what he thought, I never tried harder in my life to be the best I could be.

The Minnesota Twins won 102 games, and my old friends Don Mincher and Harmon Killebrew enjoyed their first World Series, even though they lost to Sandy Koufax and the Dodgers in seven games. Sandy recorded his fourth no-hitter in 1965 and won 26 games during the regular season, with a 2.04 earned-run average, striking out 382 batters. He also won two World Series games, with the second one on two days' rest in the seventh game. It made me pretty proud that I always hit him so well, and I'll never forget the quote he made before I hit my home run in the 1964 All-Star game. He was in the bull pen when I came up, and just as I swung he said, "Callison can hit a fastball as well as anyone I've thrown to." Before the words were out of his mouth I'd put the ball over his head in the right-field stands beyond the bull pen. Enough of 1965—it would be the first of several bittersweet years.

Yet again, it was a year of changes. Even though I insisted to Dianne that we shouldn't buy a home at this time because if you buy you're sure to get traded, we purchased our home in Glenside, Pennsylvania (where we still live). This turned out to be a good move.

Outside our world, Cassius Clay floored both Sonny Liston (for the second time) and Floyd Patterson to remain the heavyweight champion of the world and then became Muhammad Ali. Adlai Stevenson passed, and race riots raged in Watts for five days. LBJ had 150,000 troops in Vietnam and declared U.S. forces were authorized to fight. Bob Dylan, he was writing songs against social injustice such as "Blowin' in the Wind" and "The Times They Are A-Changin'."

*   *   *

Gene Mauch:

What happened in 1965? I've been asked that before. Let me put it in real simple terms. The Phillies had a manager who was so cocky, thought his players were so good, that he thought could beat anyone at any time. We made a few trades, and they didn't work out. The chemistry we had in 1964 just wasn't the same! That's baseball. It's a difficult thing to repeat, as baseball is finding out now. Maybe we were front-runners of teams and times to come.

But let me tell you about Johnny Callison. I first saw him when he was playing with the Indianapolis Indians in the American Association in 1959. I first heard about him from a Wimbledon tennis player, Dennis Ralston, who was from Bakersfield. He told me about this great football player from Bakersfield. In passing, he mentioned that the kid was a pretty good baseball player, too.

When I first saw him, what grabbed me was, here was a little man that could play the game like a big man. What I mean is that he was remindful to me of Mel Ott, a man who was a 220-pounder from his elbows to his fingers. He was a powerful, powerful kid! One of the things that always rubbed me the wrong way when someone would talk about John or Henry Aaron was that the power was in their wrists. It wasn't the wrists at all, it was the hands. The hands are what do it! It is hand action, not the wrist action, that gives off the power. The strength comes from the fingers, not the wrists. If you open your hands you can see some wild actions from your fingertips to your wrists. Anyway, Johnny had those kind of hands—that's where the power comes from and that is what separated him from the average ballplayer. I always compared Johnny to Mickey Mantle. Mickey had more bulk, but their style was pretty much the same. It is big hands and

151

forearms which create that incredible power. Johnny had both.

As a ballplayer Johnny was a free spirit. He was a "let's get after them" sort of a guy. He was the best outfielder I ever had out there. He was one special kid. Unfortunately, I'm not articulate enough to tell you just what a great kid he was, as he was so desirous of winning. He'd always been a winner and he just wanted to continue it. I guess he hated me at first, but I made him a better ballplayer by trying to take the pressure off him. When we'd go on a road trip, I'd have him at that ball park at ten o'clock every morning. I'd have him bunt, bunt, and bunt. He'd tell me that he didn't want to be that kind of a hitter, and I'd tell him I didn't want him to be that kind of a hitter either. I'd say it was a long season, and sometimes a bunt might take him out of a slump and remove some of the pressures. You know, sometimes you can take the whiteness out of your knuckles if you get a drag bunt once in a while. I'd tell him that, and he finally came to appreciate that I was right. And he beat out plenty of bunts and it was good for his head.

Johnny had the ability to become a very versatile player, and this is what I tried to work with him on. I would tell him it would make his career easier and better even if he didn't see it that way at first. Another thing, I got him to quit pulling the ball. He hated doing that, too. I mean, he hated it. Funny thing about Johnny—and all ballplayers have quirks—he thought I didn't like the way he played. I finally got through to him that I did like the way he played the game, I just wanted to help him further develop his incredible talents. He finally accepted this and came along to be the best hitter I ever had.

Fielding? He was the best. Ask anyone who followed baseball back in those days. Johnny's name should come up with Clemente, Aaron, Mays, Snider—any of them. He would be in the top ten by anyone rating outfielders who would be qualified to rate them. Johnny could read the hitters and just had that great ability to charge the ball. When I saw him in Indianapolis he could fly—he lost some of that speed with an injury in winter ball, but even so, he was extremely quick. But he learned how to outsmart a hitter or runner. I taught him to watch the third-base coach because he's the one that shuts the runner down. Johnny began working on the third-base coach (and he was a quick study), and he mastered the art quickly. He still holds the record for the most assists in one year by an outfielder, and he did it year after year.

The one thing I could never figure out about Johnny, however, was that he couldn't play left field. He was a center fielder in high school. Usually a center fielder can play anywhere. He just couldn't play left field—in right field he was awesome, which normally is a more difficult position to play. But that was Johnny—he was always special.

Clutch hitter? I could say all the right baseball cliches here, but I'd rather mention in all the years I managed Johnny Callison, and I was a bunt manager, I never put the bunt sign on with Johnny at bat with men on first and second. That's how much I respected his hitting. The worst I could ever foresee in such an at bat would be that he would get a force at second and beat the ball out at first base. I can't say that for anyone else I ever had, and that's some compliment from Gene Mauch. I knew when Johnny was up I was never going to be doubled out of an inning, and I can't ever remember that happening.

You know, where Johnny batted in the order, either number two, three, or four, it was a responsible position, and you don't put people there that aren't clutch performers. Just putting a man in those slots of the order doesn't mean he is a clutch hitter. A person that bats in these positions performs the same whether it is his first at bat or last. Whether the game is on the line or not! Johnny always approached each at bat the same. He was up there to do his best and that is why he was so special. He was a very special ballplayer.

What happened to Johnny Callison in those post-1965 years? I laugh when people ask me that question. The answer is nothing. Johnny never had a bad year. He was one of the most consistent players that ever played the game. Every year, he played the first game in April with the same dedication as he played the last game in October. He was the only player I ever managed who played the game with such determination.

There are only two things I feel badly about regarding Johnny Callison. First of all, and which will stick in my mind as long as I live, he should have been the MVP in 1964. I never saw anyone play any harder and perform as well in 162 games. If I could have figured a way to win a couple of those ten games we lost at the end, he would have had it for sure, and it would have been a good thing for Johnny emotionally and financially. I think I would give up about anything I ever accomplished to have had that happen for him. He was so deserving of the award. The other thing, I think Johnny got out of the game prematurely. If he would have been in a better atmosphere he could have played several more years and should have. In the final analysis, Johnny reached his baseball potential. No one worked harder to get as much out of himself as he did. He's a helluva man!

A final point: Johnny's wife Dianne is a helluva lady. She's so strong! She's a great lady and a good person. Give me a team of Callisons and I'll win you a pennant every year!

*   *   *

I guess being traded by the White Sox was the first time I was ever rejected in athletics. It took me at least a year to recover from that one, and I couldn't believe it when a proven star like Frank Robinson had been traded by the Cincinnati Reds to the Baltimore Orioles during the winter before the 1966 campaign. To make it worse, it was for a pitcher named Milt Pappas, who was not a star. Rumor had it though that Frank had some bad off-field incidents the Reds were not happy about. But trade Frank Robinson—how could it happen? But this was big league baseball! It was the year 1966—it would be another year of changes and life would go on.

Wilt "The Stilt" Chamberlain, all seven feet three inches of him, would break the NBA's career scoring record. Brezhnev became the Soviet leader, and Vietnam veterans would start protesting against antiwar protesters. Jack Nicklaus was the first to win two consecutive Masters, Sophia Loren wed Carlo Ponti, Frank wed Mia, and the Beach Boys were topping charts with the "Sloop John B."

The world outside seemed to be raging, with a sniper killing twelve people perched atop a tower at the University of Texas in Austin, the war raging in Vietnam, and hecklers at civil rights marches now facing bayonets. I felt much safer in my baseball world, and on August 17, Willie Mays hit his 535th home run to take second place only to the immortal Babe Ruth. On November 8th Ronald Reagan was elected governor of California, and we (men) couldn't believe the advent of miniskirts. On November 18th Sandy Koufax retired, choosing future health to be the better part of valor from permanent injury.

The 1966 campaign was even more frustrating, hectic and controversial. On July 22, 1966, I failed to catch a short fly at San Francisco's Candlestick Park. Willie Mays sprayed a loop into right, and I didn't get to it. Three runs followed, and Mauch got red hot, implying that I hadn't given the chase everything had. I told Gene that was bullshit and to go fuck himself. Gene countered, "That remark will cost you a thousand!" I fired back that I could no longer play for him and wanted to be traded. Of course, the papers made a big deal out of this incident. I eventually paid $250 of the fine, and as far as Gene and I were concerned, the incident was over. Not for the papers and John Quinn, though—it was the subject of many articles and conversations for months to come.

We didn't have a bad year in 1966. We won 87 games and lost 75. We finished in fourth place, which was an improvement over the year before. I had some nagging injuries but still managed to play in 154 games. I hit .276 but only clubbed 11 home runs. I had 55 RBIs but led the league in doubles with 40 and picked up 7 triples. Allen hit 40 home runs and batted .317. We picked up Bill

White and Dick Groat and they had good years. We even had the infamous Bob Uecker (Miller Light), who hit .208 and appeared in 76 games. Short won 20, Bunning 19, and our new acquisition, Larry Jackson, won 15. We were a good team but the quality of our competition was just so excellent.

The Dodgers won it again, with Sandy Koufax (his last year) winning twenty-seven games, ERA of 1.73, and he struck out 317. I couldn't believe it when he retired. In fact, it scared the hell out of me because he was the best at his game and retired when he was on top. It made me wonder when it would happen to me.

The Orioles swept the Dodgers four straight in the Series, and the 1966 campaign was complete. The Dodgers lost the World Series because they didn't hit. Rumors started flying that the Dodgers wanted to trade pitcher Don Drysdale for me. I couldn't conceive of the Phillies trading me, even for a great pitcher like Drysdale. The Philadelphia fans had been so good to me, and I really hoped I wouldn't be traded. My wife Dianne was beside herself concerning the rumors. I was sure Quinn was having his fun during and after the series throwing my name out to all the hornswogglers, making a big issue out of the difference of opinion Gene Mauch and I had had over Willie Mays's flare to right. I was right, too. I found out later that Ed Short of the White Sox told Quinn he'd regretted the day Bill Veeck traded me for Gene Freese. Also, other clubs were interested in me, and when Quinn finally came out and said he'd have to get three good players for me, I felt safe!

Getting back to my feud with Mauch, six days following the incident I told Gene I wasn't seeing the ball clearly. Mauch suggested that I have an eye examination. I learned I was 20-30 in one eye and 20-50 in the other. I couldn't believe how much clearer everything was when I got my first pair of eyeglasses. However, when I showed up on the field for the first time with my new steel-rimmed special tinted glasses, I took a lot of kidding from my teammates. "Those peepers help?" the other players jeered! "Damn right," I'd say—"What do I look like, Mr. Magoo?" And the glasses did help! By years end, I led the league in doubles.

The end of the season had an ironical twist as well. The Dodgers were playing us in a series that would determine whether or not they would win the pennant. In the first game of the series, I rushed back to second base on a close play, only to sprain my ankle. I was carried off the field on a stretcher, and Gene should have known me better by now. I always played every game to the hilt. We had nothing to gain by winning any of those games with the Dodgers, but I played that first game giving it my all. At season's end most players take it cool if nothing is at stake—I never did, nor did I dog it on Mays's fly ball back in July of that season. Perhaps at the time, Gene was just trying to build a fire under my ass—that was his job. I guess that is where I left it anyway, because I knew I turned as many singles into doubles as any player did during my playing days.

*   *   *

Dick Allen:

Muffy (a name Callison gave to Allen because of all the errors he made during the 1964 campaign)! He was sumbuck. He worked hard to make himself a ballplayer. I first met him during the spring training of 1961. He didn't have too much to say then, and like he was my senior. He didn't pay too much attention to me or any other rookie, but as I got to know him over the years I understand it now. He was just working on his game. He wasn't being a snob or anything like that. He just kept to himself and worked at his game very hard.

You know, Johnny and I are both Pisces. I was March 8th and he was March 12th. It takes us a while to warm up to anyone, but when we do we're alright. Another thing about us Pisces—we have the same work habits, but just might do them in different ways. Johnny was always at the ballpark by 1:00 or 2:00 P.M.—I was always late, but I had been doing the same thing he had. He'd work out on the field and I would get up at six in the morning and work out at home. When the game started we were both ready! Our statistics prove it! When I look back, I can say we just became close. What I love about him the most, to this day, is that Johnny never kissed anybody's ass. I didn't either.

The 1964 season with the Phillies was my most memorable—it was something! We did more than anyone thought we could, and because of it, players like Johnny and I began to make our mark. Johnny and I complemented each other. He hit left and I hit right. He was the man that year, though. It seemed like all the good things I did (and I was Rookie of the Year), Johnny just took it one step further. When we were in our losing streak at the end of the end of the 1964 season, I hit two home runs against the Milwaukee Braves in a game we really needed. Well, Johnny hit three that game. We still lost the game, but Johnny and I were giving it everything we had, and he was always on top. He was sumbuck! It was the "black cats" you say? No it was the buzzards. We couldn't kill nothing and nothing would die!

Johnny should have been MVP in 1964 and probably in 1965. But it doesn't work that way. When we blew the pennant we blew the MVP for Callison. It hurt! More for Johnny than losing the pennant. You see what happened over in St. Louis, they turned Lou Brock loose to run on his own. The Cardinals were always moving, and when Boyer got a hit, he had a much better chance of getting an RBI than Johnny did. We could only steal when Gene told us we could steal. So if you talk about stats, even so, Kenny Boyer only had a few more RBIs than Johnny—I attribute that to a more aggressive Cards club. Case in point, Johnny had to work much harder for an RBI. I, myself, led the league in runs scored that year with 125. I batted ahead of Johnny, so that should speak for itself how valuable he was in the clutch. Remember Willie Mays? He was second in runs scored that year—so I say again, that is how valuable Johnny was!

Sometimes I feel bad that perhaps Johnny never got the recognition he should have during those years after 1964 and 1965 and that it was because of me. We were not in the pennant running, and the press seemed to concentrate more on me because of controversy. Johnny just loved the game and he worked at it harder than anyone I knew. I don't think Johnny would ever agree with this, but I've told many people he made the most influence on my baseball career. I just watched him work at the game and he was like me that way—he made me believe in myself and in the fact that the game itself was worthwhile.

Nobody knows how difficult it is to be a professional athlete. Johnny and I went through the Philly years together and it is a tough town to play ball in. He has a great sense of humor and never catered to the reporters. He was a Phillies star, and reporters were always trying to get in his head, especially Stan Hochman. Rather than running to the reporters to get press, Johnny would just say, "Give 'em a drink." I loved that about him and he taught me a lot. I seemed to just get the press because I was more controversial off the field.

You know, people looked at me because I was this big black guy that could hit the ball further than they'd seen it hit before, and expected no less. Johnny nearly swung a bat as large as mine (he hit with a forty-ounce bat) and they never thought about it because he was so small in stature. What Johnny did most, people didn't appreciate, because they didn't really know what was going on then—other than after Callison arrived, the Phillies started being respectable. Let me tell you, he was something else. As I called him, he was sumbuck!

*   *   *

On January 15, 1967, at an only two-thirds full L.A. stadium, Bart Starr and the Green Bay Packers methodically took apart the Kansas City Chiefs 35 to 10 in the first Super Bowl. Twelve days later astronauts Virgil Grissom, Edward White, and Roger Chaffee were killed on the ground in a flash fire that engulfed their Apollo 1 spacecraft. The war in Vietnam had escalated as President Johnson emphasized that he would not stop the bombing of North Vietnam until Hanoi reduced its military actions. On May 1st, Elvis married Priscilla, and the English rock group the Beatles joined the drug culture with their new "Sgt. Pepper's Lonely Hearts Club Band."

During these times I began my tenth year of professional baseball in 1967. Although only twenty-eight years old, I was a veteran of the game now. Baseball was our way of life and we felt settled in our home in Glenside. There was still a lot of traveling, of course, but we began looking at my occupation as sort of normal. The team didn't have a bad year in 1967. We won 82 and lost 80. We finished fifth. Our players were about the same guys we had in 1966 and we all played about the same. I was hampered with some nagging injuries and only played 147 games. I hit .261, with 30 doubles and 5 triples, and cracked 14 home runs. I drove in 64 runs. Dick Allen had another good year, batting .307, and he hit 23 home runs. Jim Bunning won 17 games and Cookie Rojas added another position to his credit as he pitched one inning of shutout ball. He'd finally played every position in the major leagues. It just seemed like our guys from 1964 (and nearly all of us were still there) had just settled into where we fit. Looking back, maybe in 1964 we did just play over our heads because our Phillies years that followed were pretty consistent. We played good competitive, respectable baseball. We certainly weren't great or good, but we were a tough team to beat and a better-than-.500 club.

These were the times when I began tiring of battling with general manager John Quinn. After 1965 it was impossible to get a cost-of-living increase in salary. Frustrated, and I wasn't the only one, I just didn't feel like giving it 100 percent anymore, although I probably did physically—I wasn't there emotionally. When we'd go on a losing streak Quinn would sometimes call me up at night to rattle off about this or that. He was usually drunk and his words didn't make much sense. I just wished he'd leave me alone, and eventually I learned to just hang up because he wouldn't remember who he'd called or what he said the next day anyway. Arguing with him about money and putting up with his late-night calls actually made me sick. Baseball wasn't that much fun anymore, and I found it more difficult to get myself going every day.

For baseball, though, 1967 was an exciting year, with the great pennant race in the American League. The Red Sox, Tigers, Twins, and White Sox battled it out until the last day of the season, when Jim Lonborg defeated Minnesota's Dean Chance to win the pennant. Old friends like Norm Cash (Tigers) and Killebrew and Battey (Twins) were in the thick of it, and I must admit I wondered how my career would have gone had I stayed over in the American League.

The St. Louis Cardinals ran away with the National League by winning 101 games. Former Giant Orlando Cepeda won the MVP as he hit .325 and slugged 25 homers for the Redbirds. A young left-handed pitcher named Steve Carlton had won 14 games for them after ace Bob Gibson went down after being hit in the leg by a line drive off the bat of Roberto Clemente. The Cardinals beat the Red Sox in 7 games to win the Series, with Bob Gibson winning 3 games.

Charley O. Finley began to make his controversial mark in baseball during this campaign. Ken Harrelson, who made his way to the Red Sox after being made a free agent by Finley, called the A's owner "a menace to baseball." After the season, Finley announced he was moving his team again—this time to the city on the other side of the Golden Gate Bridge—Oakland.

Although I had seemed to hit a stride of mediocrity in my world of baseball, life outside of the game was in turmoil, full of changes. Westmoreland wanted more men in Vietnam. War protests were beginning at the Pentagon, led by peace activists like folksinger Joan Baez, who staged antidraft rallies encouraging young men to burn their draft cards. The first supersonic airliner, the Concorde, was unveiled, as was the first microwave oven.

On the lighter side, the best movies were *The Graduate* and *Bonnie and Clyde*. And if this wasn't enough to keep us sane, we could tune in the television on Tuesday night to watch "BIFF!" "BAM!" "ZOWEE!" "Holy Guadalcanal, Batman, what now?!" "Tune in next week, 'same bat-time, same bat-channel.' "

*   *   *

Lori Callison McGowan:

I wish I'd been older when my dad was playing for the Phillies. I especially wish I could remember all the trips my mother and I took together across the country to meet my father, but I don't. Even to this day, I still hear my parents tell about new experiences they had in those days.

My first recollection was while still in grade school. Every year our family left for Florida in February. I guess I didn't realize what an important man my dad was to the community, nor did I appreciate his unique occupation. I always thought of him as any other dad. You know, like having a job like mailman. But in February of each year we began preparing to leave for spring training. I got special permission to get out of school as long as I saw a tutor for an hour a day while we were south. I looked forward to every trip, and the older I got, the more I appreciated it. During six months of the year it seemed like Dad was never home. But when we were in Florida he was always there and was always doing neat things with us. He liked to take me boating and fishing. We just spent a lot of time together. They were very special times that I'll always cherish.

Mom took us to a lot of ball games during the summer. A lot of times she would meet us there, as Dad would take my sister and me with him when he left for the ballpark. He would take us into the clubhouse and all of the players would make a fuss over us. When it was time for the players to go onto the field he'd bring us to our seats where we always sat—directly behind home plate and the backstop netting. Mom always insisted that we sit there so we wouldn't get hit by any foul balls. When my sister and I got a little older, of course, we weren't allowed in the clubhouse anymore where the guys were dressing, and I missed being there.

The players and their families were like our family—one big family. As I grew up, friends and people would ask me what it was like to be the child of a big league ballplayer, and I never knew quite what to say. If there was a big game a teacher or two would tell me to wish my dad well, and some of the boys in my class would ask me baseball questions. I just didn't think about it, I guess. He was just Dad to me!

✝   ✝   ✝

On January 14, 1968, the Green Bay Packers hammered the Oakland Raiders 33–14 to win Super Bowl II, and at the end of the month the Vietnam Reds launched the Tet offensive by attacking more than 100 cities from the Mekong Delta to Saigon and north to the highlands. At the same time North Korea captured a U.S. surveillance ship, the *Pueblo*, and San Francisco's Haight-Ashbury had become a hippie haven, providing crash pads and free clothes for runaways. Rock groups such as the Grateful Dead, Janis Joplin, and the Jefferson Airplane provided rock and roll as a form of protest. Just before the baseball season was to get under way news flashed on April 5th that Martin Luther King had been assassinated in Memphis, Tennessee, which generated rioting in most major cities. President Johnson, pleading for an end to these riots, signed the Civil Rights Act of 1968 six days later, on April 11th. Yet life and baseball went on!

In 1968 the bottom began to fall out of Gene Mauch's Phillies. We finished in a seventh-place tie with the Los Angeles Dodgers, with a record of 76–86—we finally dropped below .500. Gene Mauch was fired after fifty-three games when we were 26–27.

163

George Myatt took over for two games, which we won, and then Bob Skinner took over as manager of the club for the rest of the season.

It seemed that I had my worst year with injuries. I strained the muscles in my rib cage during a good rip at a pitch, and my knee was bothering me even worse. I only played in 109 games and batted a lowly .244. I managed 14 homers but only drove in 40 runs. Dick Allen finally hit below .300 (.263), but he managed 33 home runs. Allen's .263 was the highest average on the team, and we still had Bill White, Rojas, Taylor, and Gonzalez. Lefty Chris Short won 19 games and posted an ERA of 2.93. I guess he was the only one that made us respectable.

The year 1968 turned out to be the year for the pitchers. Batting averages around the league plummeted. Denny McLain, of the Detroit Tigers, won thirty-one games against six losses. He was the first pitcher to win thirty games since Dizzy Dean did in 1934, pitching for the St. Louis Cardinals. This feat hasn't been accomplished since this writing. In the National League, Don Drysdale of the Dodgers set a record by pitching fifty-eight and two-thirds scoreless innings, and several no-hitters were thrown during the year.

The World Series matched up two teams, St. Louis and Detroit, where pitching would prevail. The series went the full seven games, and it was the Cardinals' Bob Gibson coming out on top. Bob Gibson won two games, but he struck out thirty-five batters—seventeen in game one, when he defeated McLain 4–0, giving up only five hits.

And as the world churned, so did baseball. In December of 1968, Commissioner William Eckert was fired by the club owners. Forty-two-year-old Bowie Kuhn, a Wall Street attorney, was chosen to take the helm and preside over baseball's first attempt at divisional play. Each league was divided into two six-team divisions. The schedule warranted that teams in the same division would play each other eighteen times, and 12 games were scheduled with each team in the other division. It was still a 162-game schedule, but at year end there would now be a divisional championship series (best three of five)—the two winners to go on to the World Series.

The fighting didn't stop with John Quinn either. He was still calling me at night when he had a few too many, and now he was trying to cut my salary. He was making life miserable for me in baseball, and all I could think of was getting out. Not out of baseball, but I wanted to get away from him. We had made our home and friends in the Philadelphia area and certainly didn't want to leave, but with the way the team was going and mostly his (Quinn's) antics, times were becoming unbearable. I suggested to him that he trade me—but he wouldn't do it!

I was happy to see the year 1968 end, as I'm sure others were as well. Bobby Kennedy was assassinated in June while running for the presidency. Hubert Humphrey lost a close election to Richard Nixon, who became the president-elect, while the war continued to rage in Vietnam despite the Paris Peace Talks. The Apollo 8 team of Lovell, Anders, and Borman successfully orbited the moon. I remember thinking, I wished they'd took Quinn with them and dropped him off there.

I didn't like what had happened to major league baseball as the season of 1969 approached. The league had become diluted with subpar performers because of the great expansion. There were no more batting orders that featured six or seven quality hitters. There were no more pitching staffs with four or five quality starters. It was the beginning of big changes in the major leagues as I had once known it.

Changes? On January 12 Joe Namath and his New York Jets defeated the Baltimore Colts 16–7 to win Super Bowl III. When the American Football Conference merged with the NFL, this was an event everyone was assured wouldn't happen for many years to come. In the third year, a team from the old AFL beat an NFL team for the championship. Even more remarkable was the fact that by

October of this same year the lowly New York Mets would play and beat one of the best baseball teams put together, the Baltimore Orioles, in the World Series. No! Major league sports would never be the same, nor would the world outside.

Two new teams were added to the National League—the Montreal Expos and the San Diego Padres. We were placed in the Eastern Division of the National League. This division consisted of the Mets, Cubs, Pirates, Cardinals, Phillies, and Expos. The Western Division consisted of the Braves (Atlanta), Giants, Reds, Dodgers, Astros, and Padres. The American League added two teams as well. They were the Kansas City Royals and the Seattle Pilots. The Eastern Division consisted of the Orioles, Tigers, Red Sox, Senators, Yankees, and Indians. The Western Division consisted of the Twins, Oakland A's, Angels, Kansas City Royals, White Sox, and Seattle Pilots.

I think all of us veterans were confused—too many teams. We finished fifth in our division with a record of 63–99. Only the expansion team, Montreal (managed by Gene Mauch), finished with more losses (110). Bob Skinner managed 108 games and George Myatt finished the mess off. Nagged with injuries once again, I played in only 129 games, batting, for that year, a respectable .265. I poked 16 homers, drove in 64 runs, and hit 29 doubles and 5 triples.

But the most amazing thing about that year was the New York Mets. The year before (1968) they lost 89 games and finished 9th. In 1969 they won 100 games to win the Eastern Division—I wondered how that could happen. No one will ever know, but if one would try to rationalize—it had to be the expansion and dilution of the players. Guys came up and had a big year—never to be heard from again!

The Atlanta Braves won the Western Division by winning 93 games. The year before they had split 81–81 and ended up in fifth place. The Mets took them 3 straight in the playoffs. In the American League an excellent ball club, the Baltimore Orioles, won the Eastern Division with 109 wins. Minnesota won the Western Division with 97. Baltimore beat them 3 straight. The Mets lost the first game of the World Series at Baltimore and then won the next 4 behind the great pitching of Jerry Koosman and Tom Seaver. Indeed, it was the "Miracle at Flushing Meadows." A year of the Jets and the Mets.

It was the year that Mickey Mantle called it quits. It was the year that our manager, Bob Skinner, suspended Dick Allen for a month before he himself resigned in despair at midseason. It was the year that I decided I could take no more of John Quinn and I told him I wanted out—period. Send me to the West Coast, I begged. I will not play here anymore! Sensing my sincerity, he traded me to the Chicago Cubs for Dick Selma and Oscar Gamble.

At least my years of misery with John Quinn were finally over. I felt relieved. I had wanted to be traded to the West Coast, but the thoughts of the Chicago Cubs were encouraging. First of all, they had finished second to the Mets in 1969. They had an excellent ball club and would be a pennant contender, I was certain. I was thirty years old and figured that I still had another five to ten years to play ball. I was excited, and the thought of playing day games at Wrigley Field seemed a welcome relief.

I thought about the year just passed. It was the first flight of the Concorde. Nixon was already removing troops from Vietnam. And mankind had made its greatest leap—to the moon. I thought, if Armstrong could walk on the moon, Callison could lead the Chicago Cubs to a pennant!

$$*\qquad*\qquad*$$

Cookie Rojas:

I have great respect for Johnny. He was a great ballplayer, an outstanding hitter, and a helluva outfielder with a very good arm. He was very consistent and could really run the bases. Johnny could do it all, and he did it all for us with the Phillies. I really feel badly to this day that he didn't get the MVP award in 1964. Nobody deserved it more than he did that year!

You know, in 1964 nobody gave us a chance to be a contender. But we just had the right mix of guys, and Gene was a great manager. We put together a club that was very exciting and simply executed the fundamentals of baseball well. It seemed like we just played beautifully the first 150 games. We had a 6 ½-game lead with 12 to play. I remember Johnny being the one that was still worried about us not making it, and as it turned out he was right.

Looking back, it is easier to understand what happened to us. We were a young ball club that never had this type of pressure put on us before. You also have to remember the tremendous teams we were playing against. These were the days before the quality of players per team began to get diluted. Every opponent had three, four, or five good hitters and several good pitchers. And teams like the Dodgers, Giants, Cardinals, and Reds had past experience with pennant races. We, of course, hadn't, and it would show. It wasn't even that we played poorly. Things just started to happen—crazy stuff.

We just didn't go out there for ten games and get beat. We played some helluva good ball games. We'd be ahead and then lose somehow in the late innings. A guy would steal home, a bad bounce over an infielder's head, a routine fly ball to the outfield that nobody got to. Then, the next guy up would hit a triple or a home run, winning the game for the other team, when the game maybe should have been over if a screwy play hadn't happened. I'll never forget that game against the Braves. Johnny hit three homers and Richie hit two. The Braves tied it up, and Rico Carty beat us in the last inning. But that's baseball. It is the most complex game of all—it's a round ball in a square box. I would just like to mention that we never gave up. We were always hustling, and no one did more than Johnny!

Johnny perhaps had his best year in 1965. He hit for 32

homers and over 100 RBIs. However, as a team, it is difficult to repeat a year like 1964, and we couldn't. Why? We made some trades that didn't work very well—injuries, of course. Back in those years you needed to have twenty-five players contributing. You needed great efforts from the whole team. Even so, we won 85 or 90 games, but the teams that won the pennants were winning more than 100. Eighty-five or 90 games today would win you a pennant nearly every year. It was just different in those years, and I think we played in the golden era of baseball.

The next four years (1966–1969) we just didn't get it together again. We made some bad deals, like giving up Fergie Jenkins and Culp. Our pitching was poor, and the guys that had the great years in '64 and '65 were getting older and became troubled with little injuries here and there. Like I said, even in those latter years Johnny played well. He was always very consistent. It is a difficult thing, though, to play 162 games. You become very tired and frustrated when you're not winning, and this type of thing becomes contagious on a ball club. Our team struggled the last four years Johnny and I were with the Phillies. Toward the end even Johnny was in and out of the lineup.

As a ballplayer, the thing I remember the most about Johnny was his clutch hitting. It seemed like when his at bat meant something, he'd always come up with the hit. He won a lot of games for us in the eighth and ninth innings. Only the special type of ballplayer can hit when it counts. In fact, I think Johnny would have been a .300 hitter every year if he didn't have the responsibilities he had with the Phillies. But the way our team worked, the Taylors, Wine and Rojas tried to make contact with the ball to get on base for Johnny to come up to knock us in. He was a small guy but had terrific power. Consequently, in a lot of situations he was up there to hit the long ball. Therefore, he didn't get the opportunity to hit for average. Long-ball hitters have a difficult time maintaining a .300 average because they have to swing much harder. Johnny had a lot of long outs, and, of course, when you swing hard you're going to strike out.

If Johnny would play for the Phillies today, at the Vet, God only knows what he could have done. It was a difficult thing to hit a home run at Connie Mack, especially for a left-handed hitter. Johnny hit a lot of balls off that huge right-field wall—those balls would have been out of the Vet. His power alley was to right center, and Johnny made a lot of four-hundred-foot outs. If he'd have played today he'd hit between thirty-five and forty homers a year. His average would have been much higher too, because Johnny hit the ball hard. A lot of those balls would have been too hot to handle on today's artificial turf. At Connie Mack the grass and dirt would take a lot of the velocity off the ball.

I guess when people remember Johnny Callison they talk about his hitting. In fact, the average fan really misses much of what goes on in the game. I came up as an infielder but ended up playing all nine positions in the majors. I'd never been an outfielder until I came to the Phillies. Johnny knew all of the hitters, of course, and he was constantly moving me around when this guy or that guy came up. I became a much better player because of what I learned from him. He loved baseball and really knew the game.

I was also on the other end of his throws from the outfield when I played infield positions. He had a very accurate arm and really made it easier for an infielder. The ball would usually come into us at the bag on one nice bounce. He was a helluva all-around baseball player!

Johnny was a superstar, but I never thought he got the credit he deserved, partly because he played so long in Philadelphia. We just didn't get the press like a player would in New York, L.A., or Chicago. If we had won the pennant in 1964 that would have helped considerably, too. Johnny became known nationally when he hit that home run in the all-star game, but if we'd gotten to the Series he'd have been known that much more. When we blew that pennant we cost him the MVP and had he won it, the award might have made all the difference in the world to him. I really feel badly about Johnny not winning in that year. You know, when you're just starting out in the game, you think you're going to play forever and never get old. But time passes by quickly and suddenly it is over. I, myself, always thought I'd earn a gold glove, but I never got it. To this day I rank second to Nellie Fox as the best fielding second baseman (.984). I don't think I was ever considered for the trophy, and that always hurts. But that's just the way it works.

Johnny is one of the finest people I've ever met. He was a very private kind of guy and was always very honest and open. He held malice toward none. When in the uniform he was all business. He played the game tough! After the game, he just wanted to go home to be with his family. He was very competitive but left it at the field. He was the kind of guy who would hit you a game winning homer one night and the next day he'd just be ready to go again. He'd never talk about his accomplishments the night before and loved the game—it was his living. He always gave it 100 percent. He was a player everyone could count on.

Every time Johnny and I get together we have a good time. He will always be a good friend, but when I see him I think to myself, *Johnny should still be in the game.* Maybe he doesn't want to be a part of baseball because he doesn't discuss it. However, he knows the fundamentals of the game. He could be a great help to young players coming up. I just can't believe an organization like the Philadelphia Phillies can't find a place for a Johnny Callison. He did so much for them. He still could! And the Phillies should give him that opportunity! If Johnny would want it, of course.

*   *   *

In retrospect, my years with the Phillies were my best baseball times. I guess I just didn't know it. My gloomy, introspective personality perhaps made me wary of fame. Family, friends, players, fans, and Mauch kept telling me I was attaining superstardom, but inwardly I never believed it. I wonder now what I could have done if I'd had more inner security. However, my private world of inner turmoil persisted, leaving me maybe shy of greater accomplishments.

I've always been reticent to express my opinions, but people tell me to this day how lucky I've been to have been a successful major league ballplayer. Too bad I never appreciated it—too many things happened. I grew up frustrated with my family situation, and baseball became a way out. When I think about baseball it was just something I latched onto that I excelled at. As time passed I became better and better, and when it offered me that way out, I think I took it too seriously and began expecting more from it than it had to offer.

Of all the professional sports, I believe baseball is the most difficult sport to make it in at the big league level. Even today it remains the sport that requires additional seasoning to attain a higher level. Football or basketball players can come right out of college and become an impactful player. It still doesn't work that way in baseball. Although college is providing a minor league system or training grounds, we still do not see players going from college to the Big Show. It is too big a step! It's the pitching if you're a hitter, and it's the hitters if you're a pitcher. A player needs a certain amount of time in the bush leagues to learn how to hit a good slider or to throw one. I spent little time in the minor leagues. My years in the bush were actually with the Phillies in 1960–1961. We were "bush!" Looking back, the team was horrible, and they could afford to let us have on-the-job training. In the final analysis, the early Phillies years were my preparatory years for the majors. The better the competition, one learns quickly to play on the quality level it took in those years when the teams weren't diluted with subpar major leaguers. In 1960–1961, most of us on the Phillies were minor league players playing against major league competition. In two years, several of us could play well and our team became cohesive, making a real run at the pennant in 1964. Those of us that came up with the 1960 Phillies and progressed at least through 1964 were probably front-runners of the years to come in baseball. There are so many teams in baseball at this time I can't help notice there aren't many ballplayers that are playing on the major league level that we played at in 1960. These players are just not ready, and it makes the game a poorer commodity than it once was!

About my family and friends in Bakersfield:

When I was with the Phillies, and the few years after, whenever we traveled to the West Coast a contingent would be in L.A., San Diego, or San Francisco. Whether it was my brother and his family, my mother and father, or a Don Jones, it was always special to me. I give much credit to my brother, Pete, as he always attempted to get my mother and father to attend a game when I played in California.

My dad had a difficult time with his alcoholism and made it difficult for us all. He made it especially difficult for my mother. There were times when she didn't want him to travel with her to see me play, and because of her he didn't. He worked on his alcoholism from time to time but not enough. I didn't really care if he made a game or not, either. Alcoholism is an infectious disease, and unfortunately, takes its emotional toll on the family. I loved him but I could never respect him.

My mother—I can't tell you how I loved and respected her. She had the really difficult life, having to deal with Dad. She worked while he drank and as a consequence lived poorly. But she provided not only monetarily but emotionally. She cared about all of us, and even going back to the Junior Baseball Association she would always try to attend my games. Whenever I was on a West Coast trip she'd turn up with someone. She had some cousins in the L.A. area so she had places to stay when I'd come in for a series. Sometimes she'd get quite a gang to come out to the ballpark. In fact, I had a pretty good following on the West Coast trips, as friends, relatives, and good local Bakersfield sports fans would show up to see me play.

Mom was always such an inspiration to me. I've often looked back when times were tough for me and found encouragement in how tough she had it and still persevered. If there is any particular mark I made by playing major league baseball, I would have to say it was for my mother. Here she was, with all these trials and tribulations, and her youngest son made it to the big leagues. I know now how proud she was of me, and I wish I would have told her how proud I was of her. I don't think I ever did—but I sure would now!

When she came to visit us in Philadelphia she was on cloud nine, listening to all the local color of her son's name. She was on cloud nine when reporters took the time to interview her. I guess, through my baseball, I gave her a time in the limelight, and nobody deserved it more than her. Had it not been for her self-sacrificing during my youth (allowing me to go with the Hammitts and other things), I could have really been in trouble. But she saw me through it all, and I like to think now that I saw her through a few things as well. I loved my mother very much and have the utmost respect for her.

Sloganeering bumper stickers shriek out these days that SHIT HAPPENS! A lot of shit happened to me, I've always thought. But looking back, it's just life. In fact, most of it I find amusing. I was this big deal from Bakersfield and yet I couldn't get a decent job, or any job, during the off season. I became a star with the Phillies and I got this great sales promotion position with Fleischman's Bakery (who had been in business for one hundred years). The next year they went bankrupt! I was the fair-haired boy for the Chicago White Sox and after two years I was traded! In retrospect, I worked my ass off in my baseball career, but I had it and it was a good one.

I was fortunate! How many people get to make a living at a game—especially a game they love the most. The experience of being a major league ballplayer compares to none. For a few years in Philadelphia my name was in the headlines nearly every day in

174

the papers. I traveled and met interesting people. I've been asked many times, in latter years, if I'd given up baseball for a master's degree and a $250,000-a-year salary on Wall Street. Nope! And I'm confident the man on Wall Street would rather have had my "seasons in the sun." Some of them would have, anyway!

In the final analysis, baseball is a business. It's special, however, because it is show business! We travel, and when we travel, I suppose we become like any other businessman. Funny things happen and there are thousands of experiences on the road. Some of them you tell about and some of them you don't. There is one I like to mention, however, because it is harmless, funny, and typical of what happens in our business.

There is not much to do when you're on the road except sit in a hotel room, go to the movies, or drink. Once in a while, players chose the latter. Wes Covington! There was this one series out in Cincinnati—probably 1964. Wes had had a few too many the night before, and when he arrived at the ballpark the next day Richie Allen said, "Hey, bro—you don't look so good." Wes was in the lineup and responded, "Nooooh problem!"

Well, Covington came to bat in the first inning and it was a riot. Wes had a peculiar batting stance. He held his bat real low and dangled his head over the plate for the advantage. Most of us hitters hold the bat in a position like it's a weapon to defend ourself against ninety-mile-per-hour fastballs. Not Wes! The Reds pitcher's first pitch was high and tight, and Wes couldn't move. The ball hit him square in the bean and he fell over like a tenpin. When the medical people hauled Wes off the field on a stretcher, Dick Allen looked at his teammate and chanted, "Nooooh problem. . . . Nooooh problem, bro!" Honest to God, it was funny because Wes didn't know what hit him—he was so drunk! When he woke up in the clubhouse he didn't remember being at bat.

On the same subject, as I mentioned before, about Tony Gonzalez being hit all the time. In all the years I played, from JBA up, I was never hit in the head by a ball. This past summer, Ron Perranoski was pitching an old-timer's game at Milwaukee. He was a great pitcher in his day and could snap off a curve ball better than most of them. On this particular night he threw me a ball that I expected to break and it didn't. It hit me right on top of the head, and thank God, as we get older, the balls lose velocity. I kept waiting for it to break and it didn't. Lesson learned: Old hitters can't hit; old pitchers can't break a curve anymore! I found out the hard way!

My Phillies years—the real memories are of the players. I was with the same guys (basically) for ten years. Perhaps the most difficult thing is getting traded, even when you want to be traded. There will always be special years in a ballplayer's career, and the Phillies years were mine. I matured as a "star" during this time, and the players that played with me were the ingredient that made it happen for me. We'd meet as opponents in the years thereafter, but it wasn't the same as when we were teammates. As people, we were the same, and I guess we'll always love each other!

Perhaps the real memories are of the players, not to slight the fans. I came to love the Philadelphia fans! They expected nothing from us, and when we were losers they told us. But when we performed well, the fans cheered like nobody cheered. Philadelphia fans want a winner but they don't expect one. It seemed when we almost won it, they cheered us more when we blew it than if we'd won it. To put it in a nutshell—if you give it your all, winning or losing doesn't make a difference! I gave it my all and the Philadelphia fans gave me the credit. But as a person it's the players you played with. Most of the guys I started playing with in 1960 played ball with me until I left at the end of the 1969 season. John Quinn was the difference. During my great years he wouldn't pay me! During the period after 1964–1965 he wouldn't pay me, but wanted to cut me. I'm telling you, as a ballplayer it is a difficult thing to work under these conditions, especially if you remember the past. For example, in 1961 our baby, Cindy, came down with meningitis while I was on the road. Dianne called and left a message to call home before I left Pittsburgh for San Francisco. When I called

Dianne and received the message, I asked Gene if I could go home. He agreed! In the meantime, Quinn had his wife call Dianne and she told her that she should grow up and act like a ballplayer's wife. Dianne was beside herself. Her reaction to Quinn's wife evidently earned a response from Quinn himself. He talked to Mauch. Next thing I knew I was on my way home. But wait a minute! I also had to be in the ballpark the next day to play! In San Francisco. Quinn, he was such a nice guy.

Whatever. Quinn did it to other players, too! We were home when Don Demeter's wife was having a baby. She was in labor, but Don had to leave! This was 1961, when we lost more than we won—in fact, we were so bad we couldn't win if we performed par excellence! Quinn said no! Don, if you stay with your wife, I'll ship you back to the minors!

That is the way it was in those days. You did what you were told or you were out of a job. Old man Carpenter was a great guy, but he let Quinn run the team! Quinn treated us like shit, and as a Phillie, you just lost out in those days.

We found diggings here! We loved our home, and our girls were going to school. Still, I told Quinn, trade me or else, and he did! My feelings: My seasons in the sun in Philadelphia were over. And I told myself, Callison could still make a winner in Chicago.

Chapter Seven

Chicago—the North Side of Town

The sultry nightmare was in the past. He had been an animal blistered and sweating in the heat and pain of war. He turned now with a lover's thirst to images of tranquil skies, fresh meadows, cool brooks—an existence of soft and eternal peace. Over the river a golden ray of sun came through the hosts of leaden rain clouds.

—Stephen Crane, *The Red Badge of Courage*

Twelve seasons had passed since my first year of professional baseball, beginning back in Bakersfield in 1957. Everything had gotten off to such a quick start. It slowed down for a few years, but then peaked in Philadelphia during 1964 and 1965. The past four years I'd been snake-bit with nagging injuries and my constant feuding with general manager John Quinn of the Phillies. Finally, he honored my request to be traded to the west. He sent me west, but not west enough! Here I was at the age of thirty going back to where I began, only this time it was Chicago's North Side rather than the South Side. It seemed ironic, but I was ready. Ready for a change, a new team, and an opportunity to play day ball rather than night ball with a new bunch of players who, for all intents and purposes, had every right to feel they would be a pennant contender. Leo "The Lip" Durocher was the manager, and we had players like the great Ernie Banks, Glenn Beckert, Don Kessinger, Ron Santo, Jim Hickman, and future Hall-of-Famer Billy Williams, whose bat I used to hit the home run in the 1964 all-star game. Fergie Jenkins, Bill Hands, Ken Holtzman, and Milt Pappas gave us a hell of a starting pitching rotation. I seemed to be the perfect addition for this team, who could use another power-hitting outfielder. I felt in great shape with good spirits when I headed for camp in Arizona. It seemed funny not to be going to Florida, but it felt good to be heading toward the West. The family was excited about going to a new place as well! I thought, maybe this would be the year!

I came into the Cubs' camp in excellent shape in 1970, having trimmed down to my original playing weight of 180. Even so, I was still somewhat worried about my legs. After the groin injury I had sustained in 1969, I just hoped I wouldn't run into further trouble with my wheels this season. They still twinged, but it wasn't affecting my running, and I felt great physically and emotionally. I just kept telling myself that the Cubs' chances were so good this season and was determined to do everything I could to help them win. I had one dream left—I wanted to play in a World Series. In fact, the first time I pulled on the Cubs' uniform I thought to myself, I just want to play for at least one pennant winner before I retire. It was my twelfth major league season and I couldn't have been in firmer shape or better mettle. My new teammate, Ernie Banks, was thinking the same way.

I was given the same number 6 I had worn with the Phillies for ten years. I really thought that this was it! I hated being traded and it was only the second time it had happened. I was determined this would be my last stop. I had never even thought about retiring, but I was happy to have had eleven full years in the pension fund, should the day ever come. I speculated about the days after baseball, and did some serious thinking about becoming a cattle rancher in Oregon when my career wound up. But for now, I was in the prime of life, looking forward to winning some pennants for the Cubs.

It was November 17, 1969, and I can recall answering the phone at our home in Glenside at around 4:00 P.M. A voice said, "Welcome to Chicago, John!" I responded something like, "Yeah? Who the hell is this?"

It was John Holland, general manager of the Chicago Cubs. He queried, "Haven't you heard? We've gotten you in a trade from the Phillies."

"Great! That is good news!" I said after which I held the receiver in my hand and told Dianne the news. She immediately burst into tears, realizing I had been traded. The reality of it broke a dam of emotions within her.

Dianne and I went to dinner that night to celebrate, and ironically, it was almost ten years to the day (December 8, 1959) that I had been traded by the White Sox to Philadelphia. That trade devastated me; this trade I wanted. I had kept telling John Quinn, general manager of the Phillies, to trade me. "But, please keep me in the National League! Don't send me back to the White Sox—I hate that ballpark," I would say. I left the tears to Dianne. I thought getting traded to the Cubs was a golden stroke of luck as they were a contending team of veteran players. All the home games were played during the day, and I had always hit well there in the past. In 1965 I hit nine homers in Wrigley Field alone. When I thought of other places I could have gone, I felt very fortunate.

Immediately articles started appearing in the papers. Cubs' manager, Leo Durocher, was quoted: "After Roberto Clemente, Callison has the best arm in the league. He not only adds solid defense but another big bat."

It was good to hear nice things about myself once again. I'd been in a rut in Philadelphia. My short, sweet stroke no longer popped, and I had become a mechanical robot instead of a flashing player in right field. I had lost my enthusiasm; at least John Quinn was convinced I had, and maybe he was right. I just didn't know it.

Whatever, I simply wanted out of Philadelphia. Additionally, the Phillies were rebuilding and weren't thinking of winning at that particular time. I'd been through all of this in the early sixties and such plights didn't interest me anymore. I just wanted to play with a winner one more time. I wanted to have some fun playing the game again.

I was ready for a change of scenery, and it worked. I had never hit well during spring training—it took me a while to get it all going in the past. However, my first spring with the Cubs I hit .412, 28 hits, including 6 doubles, 2 triples and a pair of home runs. I drove in 20 runs as well. It was definitely the best and happiest of spring trainings I had ever experienced. Perhaps it was a combination of things. I was still swinging like I had in the past, but the Cub players had a different attitude. There was no bullshit or any of the con stuff that I had experienced in the past. Maybe it was because of some of the unsuccessful teams I'd played with during my tenure in Philadelphia, or just playing in the shadow of Richie Allen's huge salary and publicity. I love Richie Allen to this day, but when a team isn't winning, the fans are quick to find something interesting to dwell on, and it was Richie. The fans booed him unmercifully. *But*, I thought, *at least he was getting some kind of attention—I wasn't.* I often thought if I could get some of Richie's boo birds to boo me, at least I'd feel some recognition. The Cubs' players were professional and acted like professionals. Right off, I felt at home with the ballplayers and the management. Leo said, "John's having a helluva spring. He can play and he can hit." Billy Williams was saying, "John can strap that ball," and I believed in myself once again as the season opened.

My debut with the Cubs at Connie Mack Stadium came during the first week of the season. Chris Short was scheduled to pitch for the Phillies and I knew I'd be in trouble. Shorty threw side-armed curves along with all his other good stuff; at least I knew what to expect. I came up with the bases loaded in Connie Mack and Shorty threw me one of his junk pitches, which I tapped in front of the plate to end a rally. A week later, on April 15, 1970, I came up in the same situation against Chris at Wrigley Field. I had a one-ball, two-strike count when I figured Shorty would go side-arming. And that's exactly what he did. This time I was half bailing out of the box, but managed to get the bat on the ball with a one-handed swing. The ball fell in for a double, allowing me to drive in three runs. Chris Short had nightmares about that at bat for years to come, I'm sure. But, I'd take it! The season had gotten off to a helluva good start.

Happiness was short-lived, however. It wasn't very long before Leo's colors were shown. I had been going great in April and May, when Durocher got a wild hair up his ass, deciding to platoon me. There was no reason, he just decided to do it. By mid-July 1970 I was being platooned, batting eighth in the order. I'd never hit eighth anywhere I played in my life, including grammar school, when I was playing with older kids. I became confused—I tried too hard and even reached the point where I was trying to impress Leo during batting practice. I was lousy at that, too. I started to press, trying to hit home runs. I uppercutted the ball and completely messed up my batting technique.

Leo was a strange man. He loved you or he hated you. Once he got down on you—you'd had it. I was in and out of the lineup all of the time, and there was one stretch when I didn't play for two weeks in a row. What really bugged me was that there was not a better hitter's park in the majors than Wrigley Field when the wind was blowing out. It seemed Leo deliberately played me when the wind was blowing in—never when the wind was blowing out. Durocher's logic—he wanted a big right-handed hitter to hit behind the wind.

My recollections of my first season with the Cubs (1970) were mostly of disappointments. First of all, we should have won the pennant, and it didn't happen because Leo couldn't organize his talent, plain and simple. I'd never sat on the bench before, and it was torture. I was most frustrated because I could have had a banner year if Leo would have let the normal course of events run their course. Oh well, it didn't happen, but there was a bright side to the season. My stats were good, all things considered, and I realized for sure that I could still play, and play well! During the season I'd had two four-hit games, and on August 4, 1970, I hit my 200th career home run. I thought, *maybe next year*!

Nope! I didn't have a chance to play for Durocher in 1971. I had become the forgotten man, and I was never so frustrated in baseball in my entire life. Leo just wouldn't play me. There was a month-and-a-half stretch where I didn't play at all, and, in fact, during the whole season I only had one two-week stretch when I played every day. On August 19, 1971, I was batting only a meager .195 with 3 homers and 22 runs batted in. Again, a player just can't hit if he doesn't play regularly. For some reason Leo started me one night against the Braves. Probably because a knuckleballer, Phil Niekro was pitching and everyone had a difficult time poking his medicine balls. Anyway, the game was tied 2–2 in the eighth inning when I came up with the bases loaded. I connected with a Niekro knuckler for a grand slam to win the game. The next day, I was sitting on the bench once again and I began to reflect!

I had been fed up with fighting with John Quinn in Philadelphia. I took a $2,500 pay cut in 1969. Quinn had explained to me, though, if I had a good year we could negotiate at season's end. So we did. I had hit 16 home runs that year and drove in 64 runs while playing for a very sad-sack Phillies team. I didn't have a great year, but all things considered I felt I deserved my $2,500. Instead, Quinn told me that he'd give me half of it. I was livid and said, "I'm tired of this shit—I want you to trade me!" Looking back now, arguing dollars with John Quinn beat the hell out of sitting on Durocher's bench watching my career fade away. Leo was also trying to convince me that I couldn't play ball anymore. He kept harping and harping on the fact until I was beginning to believe him and became assured that if I played another season with Leo I might never play a decent game of baseball again.

Near season's end I called general manager, John Holland, for whom I had much admiration. I asked him to trade me. He, in turn, asked me where I'd like to be traded. I told him I'd like to be near home. In fact, I told him I would like to go back to the Phillies. I thought the Phillies' new stadium (Veterans) would be a perfect place for me with that short right-field fence. I had hit only 8 home runs in 1971, but three of them were in Veterans Stadium. With this in mind, I thought John Quinn might take a chance with me, but I guess he wanted to wait until I was released. Trying to help, Holland even called Dallas Green of the Phillies, and he simply replied there were too many young outfielders in Philadelphia. That was that! It was the lowest I'd ever been. I was so frustrated I felt like giving the game up. The whole year had been a loss and I had no idea about my baseball future. I was petrified when we left for our home in Glenside after the 1971 season.

*   *   *

Dianne Callison:

It was spring of 1970 as we packed the car to the hilt and headed to Scottsdale, Arizona. It was an exciting time! Johnny was looking forward to being with the Cubs, and we were all looking forward to our winter in the sun, as we always did. This year we wouldn't have the palm trees and beaches, but we'd have the familiar sight of desert, sand, and cactus. We also looked forward to seeing friends and family, which could come visit us now from nearby California.

The Cubs were a bunch of veteran players, and it was quite easy to fit in. We had great accommodations and became good friends of the Bill Hands (a good pitcher for the Cubs). The girls were older now, and Lori was at an age (near thirteen) where we allowed her to baby-sit on occasions. It was a good change from the last trying years in Philadelphia, and everyone was optimistic about a shot at the pennant!

184

The children were thrilled to see their grandparents when they visited us. Don Jones and other friends came to see us. It was a wonderful winter and Johnny had a great spring. The teams that practiced in Arizona were all in the same area (around Phoenix), so I was able to take the children and whoever was visiting at the time to the games. It was like a new lease on life, and for the first time in a while, I looked forward to the season.

As spring training wound down, we kind of hated to leave. My good friend Dottie, from Glenside, flew out to make the trip back with me, and en route I thought that maybe the seventies would be our best years.

*   *   *

John Sletten:

I graduated from high school in June of 1962, and as the summer passed I was apprehensive about leaving home for college. As the month of August approached, I realized that it would just be a couple of weeks before I'd be off to preseason college football practice and that I'd like to get away for a while. I talked my dad into taking a trip to Chicago. We had taken only one family vacation (1959) when I was growing up, and I guess I wanted to have one more holiday before I left home for college. My father acquiesced, and away we went for a week in the Windy City.

Perhaps all real baseball fans have a proclivity to go to Wrigley Field just one time. I know I did, and when my father asked me what I wanted to do in Chicago, I told him I wanted to see the Cubs play. We stayed with army buddies of my parents, as we always did when we traveled. Dad never was big on spending money for motels and restaurants! Sure enough, Walt Kittelson (the army buddy) secured box seats behind the visitors' dugout in the second or third row at Wrigley Field for a game against the San Francisco Giants. I was thrilled!

There is not a bad seat in Wrigley Field—it's a fan's ballpark.

Within a few feet I was watching Willie Mays swinging a bat in the on-deck circle right in front of me. The Giants were in town and not only Mays but Cepeda, Pagan, Davenport, and Harvey Kuenn! Jack Sanford pitched that day against Bob Buhl. The Giants won 103 games that year and Willie Mays hit 49 home runs, and I saw one of them that day. Ernie Banks was in his prime then. He hit 37 homers that year, and hit one that day. Billy Williams, George Altman, and Ron Santo were also excellent ballplayers for the Cubs that year. It was a great thrill—one I'll never forget.

En route to Chicago, which is about five hundred miles from Minneapolis, I did some research on the Cubs and Wrigley Field. I was surprised to learn that they were first known as the White Stockings, making their debut on May 10, 1876, in a rickety wooden park on the west side of Dearborn Street between 23rd and 24th streets. In 1877 the White Stockings constructed Lakefront Park, located south of Randolph Street between Michigan Avenue and the Illinois Central Railroad tracks. The team won pennants at Lakefront Park in 1880, 1881, and 1882, featuring such popular favorites as Adrian (Cap) Anson and Mike (King) Kelly. Happy with three consecutive pennants, the White Stockings enlarged Lakefront Park to ten thousand seats. This move gave Lakefront Park the largest seating capacity in baseball at the time. There were eighteen rows of private boxes with curtains and armchairs, and it was the rage of the local sport scene. But in 1885 the popularity of the team and baseball in general forced the team to move to West Side Park at Congress and Throop streets. The club was managed now by Cap Anson. They were nicknamed the Colts. The Colts won pennants in 1885 and 1886. This would remain home until 1893, when they were required to move because of the Columbian Exposition.

Their next stop would be at the corner of Polk and Lincoln (now Wolcott), which they called the West Side Grounds. It had a double-decked grandstand that accommodated 16,000 people, featuring small balcony boxes atop the grandstand between first and third bases. After the resignation of manager "Pop" Anson in 1897, the club was known as the Orphans, because the players missed Anson. But in the year 1900 they adopted the name of Cubs. The Cubs are the only National League charter club still operating in its original city.

At West Side Grounds the Cubs won four pennants (1906, 1907, 1908, 1910). The Cubs lost the 1906 Series to their crosstown rivals, the White Sox, after winning 116 games that year. The Cubs won the World Series in 1907 and 1908, defeating the Detroit Tigers. But in 1910 they lost to the Philadelphia A's, and after that, the New York Giants ran off with three consecutive pennants.

In 1914 the Cubs were fighting the White Sox and the Whales of the Federal League, a self-proclaimed major circuit, for the rights to the Chicago sports dollars. When the Federal League folded, Whales owner Charles Weeghman acquired the Cubs as part of a peace settlement. In 1916 the club was moved in Weeghman Park at Clark and Addison streets. The park was soon renamed Cubs Park and, after William Wrigley, Jr., gained control of the club in the 1920s, it was renamed Wrigley Field. The Cubs played their first game in their new home on April 20, 1916.

In the early 1920s Wrigley moved back the stands several feet so that the seating capacity could be increased to twenty thousand. He also made park renovations designed to provide the best in comfort and beauty. In the late 1920s the stands were double-decked, raising the capacity to forty thousand. In so doing, the playing area was lowered several feet. In the late 1930s Philip K. Wrigley, who had taken over from his father, constructed bleacher seats. The following year wider chairs were installed in the boxes and grandstand. This move added to the fans' comfort but it reduced the park capacity by several thousand seats. Shortly before World War II, the tiers in the left-field stands were circled so that all seats faced home plate. Also, the box seat deck extending from left field to first base was torn down and replaced with a new box seat deck of monolithic reinforced concrete.

During the winter of 1950 and 1951 work on the right-field wall was completed. The box seat tiers in right field were circled so that the seats faced home plate. Additionally, new chairs, wider and more comfortable, were installed in the upper box seat deck. When all these renovations were completed, the new park capacity had been reduced to 36,755. Distance to the fences were 355 feet to left, 353 to right, and 400 to center, with ivy vines adorning the outside walls.

It was that day, on the way to Chicago, in the summer of 1962, that my dad first told me about the Babe's "called shot" in the 1932 World Series off the Cubs' Charlie Root at Wrigley Field. He explained to me Babe's account. He had taken two strikes, and after each one he'd held up a finger and said, "That's one! That's two!" Then he waved to the fence. Dad's analysis: "Babe was intimidating Root into throwing him another strike. That Ruth was a showboat, and he did enjoy showing a pitcher up. Sure enough, Root came in with a good one, and when Babe took his cut the ball took off like a golf ball tagged with one of Sammy Snead's best swings. It went right through a tree in center field that was filled with little boys. The Cub fans howled at the Bambino and threw all kinds of debris at him as he rounded the bases, laughing like hell. He was the Sultan of Swat!" Dad concluded, laughing himself about the memory.

Dad continued his reminiscing by telling me how Gabby Hartnett, the Cubs catcher that day, and Bill Dickey, the Yankees catcher, used to argue about the shot. Gabby said that "Babe waved his hand toward our bench on the third base side. One finger was up," he said quietly, "and I think only the umpire and I heard him say, 'It only takes one to hit.' Then, Root came in with a fast one, Babe swung, and it landed in the center-field seats. Babe didn't say a word after the home run. If he had pointed out at the bleachers, I'd be the first one to say so."

Bill Dickey would argue: "I knew the true story. I was in the on-deck circle with Gehrig at the time. Gabby always says, 'Ruth didn't point.' I say, 'Oh, yes he did, Gabby. Oh, yes he did.' And Gabby would get so mad he couldn't see straight."

I asked dad what he thought. "Well, John," he said with a laugh, "I listened to the game on the radio with my dad. I was only ten at the time. Your grandpa told me that the Babe sure as hell did call it! That was good enough for me, and it is certainly the way we all like to remember it!"

Another thing I learned on that trip was about the scoreboard situated atop the center-field bleachers. It was constructed in 1935 under the direction of a young Cub executive named Bill Veeck. The Wrigley Field scoreboard is twenty-seven feet high and seventy-five feet long, operated by hand, providing inning-by-inning scores of all major league games, as well as pitching changes. Not until 1982 was any electronic device put there to assist this operation. And I would learn that after a game, passersby outside the stadium could determine if the Cubs won or lost, depending on the flag that flies from the center-field pole. A victory is denoted by a blue flag with a white "W"; a white flag with a blue "L" denoted a loss.

I remember asking Dad that day at the game why Wrigley Field didn't have any lights for night games. This was twenty-seven years ago at the time of this writing, and I remember as though it was yesterday. He said, "I recall 1941 when there were blurbs in the paper that equipment had been purchased and towers were about to be erected to put lights in the stadium. But when the Japanese attacked Pearl Harbor, the Cubs donated the towers, the lights, and the cables to the government, who utilized the materials in the shipyards."

When we left Wrigley Field that day I remember looking back at the sign that hovered over the main entrance:

WRIGLEY FIELD
HOME OF THE
CHICAGO CUBS
GAMES START ONE THIRTY

I would have given anything to have had the opportunity to play just one game in a place filled with such rich tradition!

*   *   *

We had a great team and should have won the pennant and maybe the whole thing in 1970. It was Leo's fault! Durocher was sixty-five at the time, and he just didn't do it right anymore. He was a very charming guy and in a way you couldn't help liking him. His problem, I always thought, was that he listened to too many people! He was always playing hunches and just could never get the right players out there at the same time. For instance, even though Ernie Banks was on his way down, he still could have helped the team a lot, but Leo didn't like Banks. Banks should have been our leader—it would have been a perfect time for the Hall-of-Famer to help us put together a pennant winner. No! He didn't want to play Banks. Ernie played 50 percent of the time, and Leon platooned him with Joe Pepitone (who batted left). Joe was a good guy, who achieved some stardom with the Yankees, but he worked against the team. He wore long hair and big boots. He was the first ballplayer to blow-dry his hair. He was a maverick who was more interested in his antics than with winning a pennant. We had Williams in left, Hickman in center, and I was in right. I got off to a great start, hitting eight homers early in the season, and someone asked Durocher if he was going to play me against lefties. I knew then I was going to be platooned thereafter, and sure enough, that is what Leo did despite the fact that I'd asked Durocher to check my Phillies statistics against left-handed pitching. I hit lefties better than right-handers. My average soon dropped from .300 to .260. Eventually, he started playing me full time again, and I hit at a .280 clip and was getting my homers again. But the damage had been done!

About Leo? I tell people to this day I hated him! I guess everyone who's been interested in sports and is still living knows the legend of Leo Durocher. Everything I've read, heard from other players, and observed firsthand seems to be true.

Durocher grew up in a seedy tenement in West Springfield, Massachusetts. He worked in a battery factory, supplementing his income as a pool hustler. Quickly, he developed an unsavory reputation by hanging out with low-level mob guys and card sharks. He signed with Hartford in 1925 and was not there long before teammates, who hung their clothes on nails during the days, began finding money missing from their billfolds. Since this never occurred before Leo joined the team, it didn't take Dick Tracy to catch him red-handed spending a marked bill. Hartford was in the middle of a pennant race, so the manager convinced the team to let him stay until the season was over, promising he'd get rid of him. So they did, and Hartford won the pennant with Durocher's help, after which he was sold to the New York Yankees.

Leo couldn't hit a lick, but he was a quick, agile shortstop who was a fiery leader. He made the Yankees in 1928 but irritated the veterans by sporting flashy clothes and strutting around. Some of the players started calling him "Fifth Avenue."

Leo soon became known as a ruthless type, and during the off season he lived in California, courting movie starlets. He married Lorraine Day, and while married, boasted about dating other Hollywood bombshells.

Durocher showed no deference to anyone, including the game's proven stars. In one game against the Detroit Tigers, Ty Cobb rounded second, and as he stood poised waiting to make his next move, Durocher gave him a hip. Cobb, who may have been the fiercest, toughest competitor ever to play the game, threatened that he would "get" Durocher. Durocher opened his mouth wide, indicating he would shove the baseball down Cobb's throat. Durocher then screamed, "You're an old man. The game has passed you by. You ought to get out."

Babe Ruth, who liked almost everyone, hated Leo. Once, when Ruth lost his watch, he accused Durocher of stealing it.

191

Durocher called the Babe "that baboon," and in retaliation caught Ruth off guard in the clubhouse, knocking him into the locker. Ruth would have killed him if he could have gotten his hands on him, but Leo did it so quickly that he got other players between him and the Babe and the scene ended.

No matter where Leo was, he continually wrote bad checks and never covered them. He just seemed to get away with things because certain managers and owners liked his competitive style.

Durocher was known to also have taken the credit when credit wasn't due. He would always find blame in someone else when the blame was his. For example, Pete Reiser, the great Dodger outfielder, was his. Willie Mays, the great Giant outfielder, was his. Losses? He always had one guy picked out that lost the game! He never protected a player! Leo? He was a hard guy to like or put up with! I hated him! He shortened my baseball career by two or three years! About Leo? Well, I can say I played for one of the real assholes of the game.

*   *   *

Dianne Callison:

After spring training the girls and I returned to Glenside until the school year ended. We had decided that we'd move to Chicago for the summer. The day before the girls and I departed, I called Johnny to tell him we should be in around game time and asked him if we should come right to the ballpark. I'd been studying the map and felt pretty confident that I would arrive without too much trouble. Johnny laughed and said, "You're going to come to the ballpark with a packed car, three girls, two dogs, and the birds? No, you better go right to the apartment." Looking back, I can't believe how nice the players' wives have it today. They don't have to pack—the players can afford to rent beautiful places. We went through a lot of hardships those days.

I thought I'd examined the map to perfection, but with

children crying, dogs barking, and parrots squawking in the car one's attention gets distracted. I was dead on Chicago, I thought, when I saw the sign, WELCOME TO WISCONSIN. I turned around and finally found the apartment Johnny had secured for us for the summer. When we drove up I just let the dogs and children out of the car. I was exhausted! Johnny was staying with two other ballplayers, and when we arrived they were taking it easy watching television and drinking beers. Our youngest German shepherd (about eight months) ran right through the screen door. I guess she heard Johnny's voice, and the incident was funny after the initial shock. Johnny simply said, "I guess my wife is here!" I was ready to scream!

That summer was nice. It was as though we had a normal family life when the team was home. The guys played ball during the day, and after the game, we'd stop to get a couple of six-packs and just take our time going home with the rest of the working people. It made us seem like normal folks! Even if I didn't go to the game, it was nice to have Johnny home at a normal time.

We had a real family life that summer. We lived near O'Hare Airport at the Crestmont Apartments. We were able to have barbecues and be with our friends in the evening. It was a good time, and I envied families whose husbands played with the Cubs for so many years just because of the day games.

*　　*　　*

Cindy Callison Moore:

I wish I could remember more about my dad's baseball career because everyone tells me so much about it. I do remember when he was with the Cubs. Lori and I would babysit for the Bill Handses. I guess Lori was really babysitting for me too, but I thought I was babysitting. It was a wonderful time. Dad was always home and I wasn't used to him being there. It was nice because he would do a lot of things with us. He was a good father! Of course, Mom was always there!

I remember spring training the most. It was great to get out of school and go to Florida, Arizona, and back to Florida when Dad was with the Yankees. Teachers and some of the boys would ask me about the baseball, but I never thought a lot about it. I just thought baseball was his job, and it was! It's kind of neat when you get older and really understand how important he was to the general population when he was playing ball. He always has been and always will be to me! Yeah, I guess I'm pretty proud he was a ballplayer! I realize now, not too many kids have a dad who played major league baseball.

*   *   *

We didn't have a bad year. We won 84 and lost 78, but like I said, if Leo had kept us as a cohesive unit rather than platooning everyone, I think we would have won it. The Pirates won our division with 89 wins, leaving us in second place, 5 games back. I think Leo's decision with Banks was the big mistake. Ernie only played in 62 games yet he hit .252, 12 homers, and 44 RBIs. Banks was well respected—he should have been allowed to lead us. Glenn Beckert hit .288; Santo had a good year when he hit .267, 26 homers, and 114 RBIs. Jim Hickman had a great year, hitting .315, 32 homers, and 115 RBIs. Billy Williams hit for .322, 42 homers, and 129 RBIs. Callison, well I think I could have had my best year ever if it hadn't been for Leo's bullshit. I hit .264, 19 homers, and 68 RBIs. Fergie Jenkins won 22 games, Hands won 18, Holtzman 17, and Pappas 10. We had three guys that scored more than a hundred runs (Williams 137, Hickman 102, Kessinger 100). Beckert scored 99, Santo scored 83, and I scored 65. We scored more runs than anyone that year and we couldn't win the pennant. Thank you, Leo!

The Phillies finished fifth with another losing season. The Reds, who won the Western Division, beat the Bucs three straight in the play-offs. Baltimore took Minnesota out three straight in the

American League play-offs. Minnesota won 98 games, but the Orioles won 108 games under Earl Weaver, having three 20-game winners in Mike Cuellar with 24, Dave McNally with 24, and Jim Palmer with 20. For the Twins, Killebrew smashed 41 home runs, Tony Oliva hit .325, and a new guy, Rod Carew, batted .366 in 46 games.

The Orioles won the World Series in five games when Brooks Robinson had an incredible series both afield and at bat. The three big pitchers won a game apiece.

The seventies had begun. Little did I know how much the world, baseball, and my life would change. It started with Bud Grant's heavily favored Vikings getting vanquished by the Kansas City Chiefs 23–7 in Super Bowl IV. Abbie Hoffman and his group were found not guilty in Chicago for inciting a riot at the Democratic convention two years before. The army was accusing Captain Ernest Medina and four others of murder and other crimes at My Lai in the Vietnam conflict. Gypsy Rose Lee died and Mc-Cartney split—breaking up the Beatles. In May of 1970, National Guardsmen fired into a crowd of Kent State University student protesters, killing two women and two men and wounding eight others. Thousands of homosexuals protested in New York, and Janis Joplin died of a drug overdose. Charles de Gaulle died on November 12. TV had "M*A*S*H" poking fun at war, while George C. Scott was unforgettable in the movie *Patton*.

In baseball it was the demise of back-to-back Cy Young Award winner Denny McLain. He lost it all. He lost his money, his good name, and his sneaky fastball. Commissioner Bowie Kuhn suspended McLain for a number of incidents because of dealing with gamblers during the 1967 season. He was reinstated on July 1st, but he had lost it as a pitcher. He was suspended again on September 9th, for the duration of the season for carrying a pistol, which was in violation of the probationary conditions set by Kuhn. And at season's end the Tigers hastily unloaded McLain in a large trade with the Washington Senators.

Meanwhile, Curt Flood was busy presenting his antitrust suit against baseball. When Flood was traded by the Cardinals to the Phillies during the winter, he refused to report. In lieu, he filed suit against baseball's reserve clause, which bound a player forever to whatever team held his contract. Flood was denied his suit and sat out the season. Flood ended up joining McLain as a member of the Senators after they acquired his "reserve" from the Phillies and after he was assured the move would not hurt his case.

Bowie Kuhn had a host of problems as the seventies began. The Seattle franchise was bankrupt and was shifted to Milwaukee four days before the season opened. Houston pitcher Jim Bouton published *Ball Four*, revealing hidden personal aspects of major league baseball. Kuhn had to face a one-day strike by major league umpires during the play-offs. Indeed the sixties had passed, and maybe the seventies would be more complicated! It appeared that way to me because I didn't how I could put up with another year of Durocher.

*   *   *

Don Jones:

I was surprised when I met Johnny in Arizona during the spring of 1971. He had always been so enthralled with baseball since the day I first met him. But he told me that he found it harder and harder each day to get up for practice, games, or anything concerning baseball. I shrugged it off at the time and enjoyed visiting with him when he was playing for the Cubs.

Johnny took me into the Cubs' clubhouse after an exhibition game, and suddenly I found myself standing with Ernie Banks, Billy Williams, Ron Santo, and, of course, Johnny. When we left the clubhouse I'll never forget all the kids and fans that were waiting for us outside. They recognized the others, but they also thought I was a ballplayer. While they were waiting in line to get the stars' autographs they started asking me for mine. I didn't know what to do—I looked at Johnny and he said, "Just sign it!"

"Sign what?" I said, feeling foolish.

Johnny said with that laugh of his, "Yogi Berra! Sign Yogi Berra! They won't know the difference!"

So, I did! What the hell!

I spent the good part of a week with Johnny and his family during that spring training. I enjoyed watching him with his children and I could tell he really enjoyed them. Sherri was just a little girl. We'd be in the stands watching the game, and it seemed Sherri enjoyed just running around the bleachers. I'll never forget, though, every time Johnny was announced at bat, no matter where Sherri was, she'd come running back to sit with us during his up. It was a cute thing, and it made me feel good about my friend.

*   *   *

The year 1971 started out with the Baltimore Colts defeating the Dallas Cowboys 16–13 with a last-minute field goal in Super Bowl V. Rolls-Royce, Ltd., declared bankruptcy in February. In March, Lt. William Calley was convicted of killing twenty at My Lai. Joe Frazier outpointed Muhummad Ali to retain his heavyweight title, giving Ali his first defeat, and on July 6th Louis Armstrong, the jazz virtuoso, died. On September 8th the $70 million John F. Kennedy Center for the Performing Arts opened to the strains of a modern, haunting "Mass." Bernstein's "Mass." On the other side of the music world, Led Zeppelin surpassed the Beatles in popularity when they cut their fourth album, featuring "Stairway to Heaven."

Perhaps the baseball world was more tumultuous this year. With the Washington Senators, Denny McLain flopped to a 10–22 mark, Curt Flood jumped the team after only 13 games while his antitrust suit was pending before the Supreme Court. Owner Bob Short added the coup de grace by moving the financially troubled club to Arlington, Texas (Texas Rangers), after the conclusion of the season. Baltimore ran away with the American League East and beat the up-and-coming Oakland A's three straight in the championship series. The San Francisco Giants hung on after a serious chase by the Dodgers in the National League West, only to be defeated by the Pittsburgh Pirates in four games in the championship series. Pittsburgh defeated Baltimore in seven games to win it all.

We finished third, winning 83 and losing 79, leaving us fourteen games behind the Pirates. It was a frustrating season dealing with Leo and his platooning. I appeared in only 89 games and was constantly begging Durocher to trade me. I hit only .210, with 8 homers and 38 RBIs. I was only thirty-two years old and frustrated as hell.

Dianne and the girls spent the summer with me in Chicago again. However, as the season progressed, I found myself just hoping Durocher would trade me. Billy Williams, Joe Pepitone, Fergie Jenkins, and Milt Pappas had great years, and Ernie Banks, tired of Durocher, too, played his last season, appearing in only twenty games but still managing to hit three homers. He was one of the all-time great ones!

As it happens in the autumn of a career, another change was to take place. I was traded to the Yankees for a pitcher named Jim Aker. And for Leo, he made ninety games with the Cubs the following year before he was fired again!

I guess Chicago wasn't meant to be Callison's kind of town. Rather, it turned out to be a place for great beginnings and uncertain endings.

Chapter Eight

Yankee Pinstripes

A hero ventures forth from the world of common day into a region of supernatural wonder: fabulous forces are there encountered and a decisive victory is won: the hero comes back from this mysterious adventure with the power to bestow boons on his fellow man.
—Joseph Campbell, *The Hero with a Thousand Faces*

I think every young boy, especially those that grew up during the late forties and early fifties, dreamed of playing a game in Yankee Pinstripes in the Bronx. I know I did.

It wasn't until mid January, 1972 when I was informed I'd been traded by the Cubs to the New York Yankees in a conditional deal. The conditions were the Yankees, by May 1, 1972, must send a player, make a cash settlement, or I would be returned to Chicago. I immediately realized that I was being treated just one step above an outright release. It was difficult to believe I could be involved in such an unflattering transaction. What a comedown. It was less than five years ago that Walter Alston, manager of the Dodgers, had called me the best fastball hitter in the National League. I wondered how this could be happening to me. I was thirty-two, and for all intents and purposes should have been in the prime of my career. Now I would just sit around and wonder if I would be able to fit in with the Yankees in 1972. Worse yet! I had to make the team and there was nothing I could do about it. It was like starting all over again, and I could not believe how my career was turning out.

Everywhere I went people used to know me. Suddenly, after spending two years with Leo Durocher, I'd become an unknown. The only consolation was that if I'd spent one more year with Leo my career would have vanished altogether.

I hated changing leagues, knowing the umpires call the balls and strikes different, facing pitchers I hadn't seen before, and mostly because I wouldn't know anyone. Once reality set in, however, I became determined to become a real Yankee. I placed myself in a great frame of mind, and as a result, had a great spring. Suddenly, I found myself happy, once again, standing behind the batting cage needling my ex-Phillies teammate, Bill White (who is now President of the National League), when he'd pitch batting practice from time to time. I'd jump in the cage, out of turn, laughing as my new teammates would chase me away. I was having great fun. I loved manager Ralph Houk and really respected him. I was with a team that had a chance to win our division, and in a city so close to home that I decided to commute. The ballpark was tailor-made for me with the short right-field fence. I began thinking I could be a big deal on this club—Durocher, this wouldn't be your first mistake!

By May 1st the Yankees sent pitcher Jack Aker to the Cubs, finalizing the deal. On May 9th I belted my first home run as a New York Yankee. It was a 396 foot blast into the rightfield bull pen to beat the Minnesota Twins and Bert Blyleven, 5–3. Once again, I was off to a great start.

I'd been out of the American League for more than a decade when I returned to Yankee Stadium. I'll never forget the first trip when I was just up with the White Sox. It was mystical at that time. But I was returning now as a seasoned veteran! It was sad as I was getting older, but still there was something special about being at "The House That Ruth Built." Even though the grand old ballpark was worn down, I could still feel the presence of the great ones that once played on this hallowed ground. I could hear haunting echoes of the fans cheering Ruth, Gehrig, DiMaggio, and Mantle. Here I was, Johnny Callison, in the twilight of my baseball years, donning a New York Yankee uniform. I was proud and hopeful that I might make a mark here, too.

I had been unhappy with Leo Durocher. He wouldn't allow me to play enough, and I expressed my discontent. At first Leo really liked me. I don't know what happened, but, at any rate, I was traded to the Yankees for pitcher Jack Aker. I should have known then, and I guess I did, that I was in trouble because Jack didn't have great major league credentials. He had a ten-year career piling up only 47 wins against 45 loses. He bounced around between a lot of teams. Nevertheless, I was off to New York not knowing what to expect other than I kind of liked the idea of going back to the American League.

So, off to Fort Lauderdale! We rented a house in an area that accommodated mostly older folks. We were accustomed to Florida by now, but Fort Lauderdale was the place where all the movies were made in the sixties, etc., and it stood up to its reputation. It was simply beautiful. Where we lived we had ducks, geese, and other wildlife that seemed to find their diggings. The children loved feeding the ducks, much to the dismay of the year-round inhabitants. When you're kind to animals they seem to hang around. We were constantly chastised by our neighbors. "If the kids weren't feeding the poultry they wouldn't leave their residue on the sidewalks. You won't be back here next year, I'll guarantee you!"

We had a good time despite them! I found opportunities to take the girls fishing, and once again I had a great first spring training with the Yankees. It's funny, I still felt like a complete ballplayer and was anxious to see what I could do in the American League where I began! It felt great to be a New York Yankee!

When I arrived in spring training in 1972, the Yankees were a mediocre ball club. All the big names were gone! Ron Blomberg was playing first, Horace Clark was at second, Gene Michael played short, with Celerino Sanchez at third. Bobby Murcer (the new next Mickey Mantle) was in center field, Roy White was solid in left, and I seemed set for right field. Thurman Munson was a leader behind the plate. Lefties Fritz Peterson and Mike Kekich teamed with righties Mel Stottlemyre and Steve Kline for the starting pitching rotation. Sparky Lyle and Rob Gardner looked pretty good in the bull pen. Ralph Houk was the manager who was hopeful of finishing better than the previous year's record of 82–80.

It was a strange season. Just before we broke camp in the spring, Mets manager Gil Hodges was struck with a fatal heart attack. At the same time, the ballplayers from all teams walked off the field on strike because of certain issues, mainly the conditions of our pension plan. The strike lasted thirteen days into the season, and eighty-six games were scratched from the regular schedule. We won out over the owners, but we lost in the Supreme Court when it finally ruled against Curt Flood's 1970 reserve clause lawsuit. Little did we know what Curt Flood had done, and this first strike would begin to change baseball dramatically. Our first protests would be the front-runner of the good things that would benefit the players in the very near future.

During the winter of 1972 Willie Mays was traded to the New York Mets, and my friend Dick Allen went from a good year with the Dodgers over to the White Sox. When the season got going the American League East seemed a division of parity. The Tigers, Orioles, Red Sox, and us (Yankees) ran neck and neck until mid-September. But in the stretch run, it came down to the Tigers and the Red Sox, with Detroit finally winning it by one game, beating Boston at Detroit two out of three in the last series of the season.

All things considered, I had a good year. I played in ninety-two games, hitting .258, 9 homers, and 34 RBIs. I had several game-winning hits for the Yanks. For some reason, once again, I was platooned with a switch-hitting kid named Rusty Torres. He must have been a better left-handed hitter because, batting right most of the time, he hit poorly with a .211 average, three homers, and thirteen RBIs. Bobby Murcer had a great year, belting 33

202

homers, knocking in 96 runs and batting .296. Roy White and Thurmon Munson had good years, as did pitchers Peterson, Kline, and Stottlemyre. We finished in fourth place 79–76, but we were in the thick of it until mid-September.

As I did every year, when I wasn't at bat or in the outfield, I watched the goings-on in baseball and the world outside the game. Perhaps I had more time to reflect on things this year than any other. Because of the children's schooling, our home in Glenside, and the close proximity of New York, we decided I'd commute to and from New York during the home stands. This was difficult, especially with the night games, but I got used to it. When the White Sox came into town, however, Dick Allen would often ride home with me. We discussed a lot of things, and I looked forward to the Sox coming to town. Dick had a great year in 1972. He hit .308 and led the league in homers with 37, RBIs with 113, and walks with 99. They battled Charley Finley's moustached Oakland A's down to the wire, but finished in second place five games out. Dick won the MVP award in the American League for his efforts.

Outside the game, 1972 started out with Roger Staubach's Cowboys routing Miami 24–3 in Super Bowl VI. The hit movie *The Godfather* opened, starring Marlon Brando, and Richard Nixon made his historic visit to China. Following his trip to China, Nixon visited Brezhnev in Russia, continuing a year of firsts for U.S. diplomacy. When the presidential campaign began, candidate George Wallace was shot by a stalker in Laurel, Maryland. A month later five men were arrested and charged with breaking into the executive quarters of the Democratic National Committee in the Watergate apartment complex in Washington, D.C.

B-52s continued bombing the hell out of North Vietnam as two former White House aides, E. Howard Hunt and G. Gordon Liddy, were indicted on charges of breaking into the Democratic national headquarters in the Watergate complex. Meanwhile, on October 3rd, Nixon signed an arms limit treaty in the East Room of the White House with Soviet Foreign Minister Andrei Gromyko.

Just a few days and a month later Richard Nixon won the presidency by a landslide.

The year ended on a sad note. On Christmas Day a huge earthquake leveled Managua, Nicaragua. On December 26th, "Give 'em Hell" Harry Truman died in a Kansas City hospital at the age of 88. On December 31st, Roberto Clemente, who had gotten his 3,000th hit before the 1972 baseball season ended, was killed in a plane crash while en route to Managua to help the earthquake victims.

Oh yes, and Finley's crazy A's won the 1972 World Series by defeating the Tigers in a thrilling best three of five League championship series and then defeating the Cincinnati Reds in a seven-game series which included six one-run games. As for the Phillies, they finished dead last, winning only 59 games. But on a high note, a left-handed pitcher named Steve Carlton had 27 of those 59 wins. Also, names like Bowa, Money, Luzinski, Boone, and Schmidt started showing up regularly in their lineup. Who are those guys?

*　　*　　*

Dianne Callsion:

I guess my heart found a home in Philadelphia. Johnny wanted to be traded in 1969 and I couldn't blame him. He'd done so much for the Phillies, and other than 1964 and 1965, his efforts seemed to be unappreciated by management. He was constantly fighting with Quinn, which wasn't Johnny's nature, and it tore him apart. So off to Chicago we went.

Mr. Holland, the Cubs' general manager, couldn't have been nicer to us. He signed Johnny right away for about the same money, and he even gave us that $2,500 under-the-table bonus that Quinn (who, of course, failed to mention it to Holland) gave us each year for spring training expenses. Even though Johnny played well for the Cubs at first, Leo took it away from him. Johnny was unhappy and wanted to be traded again.

But let me regress a little bit. I'll never forget when Johnny came home complaining about a play—it was so unlike him. He never took the game home with him. Jim Hickman, who had a terrific year in 1970, was playing center field. He was a great hitter but wasn't the best in the outfield. There was a long fly ball to right center and Johnny moved over to make the catch. Suddenly, someone yelled from the stands, "I got it!" Johnny stopped and the ball fell for a triple. When something like that happened, Leo had to blame someone—he blamed Johnny. One day, Johnny went to pinch hit. Leo said as he left the dugout, "Don't strike out!" Of course, with that kind of instruction, Johnny struck out! Leo was all over him. Another time Leo went right behind Johnny's back to the newspaper to send a negative message. Johnny was in the beginnings of a slump. He was zero for seven or eight and had probably struck out during four of those at bats. Johnny always felt bad when he didn't play well, but for the next day in the papers Leo had been quoted as looking for a new right fielder. What got Johnny upset about was Durocher would never say anything to him up front—it was always behind the back and underhanded. I remember my husband, who hardly ever complained, saying, "Leo's trying to run me out of baseball!"

Johnny, by his nature, always needed positive reinforcement—not negative. He wasn't with the Cubs long before he was begging Durocher to trade him!

The Yankees were a class organization much like the White Sox. Ralph Houk was a man that you could only respect. Johnny won a game with a pinch hit one day. I never thought much about it, other than I heard it on the radio, and I was happy for him. The same day the Yankees sent me a dozen yellow roses! It never happened before and I was impressed. Johnny couldn't believe it when I told him about it.

Yes, times changed when Johnny went to the Yankees. Perhaps I thought his career would go on forever. I probably never thought much about it. The girls were older and I had a whole new set of problems trying to keep them in line. Consequently, I wasn't as much a part of the Yankee family as I had been with the White Sox, Phillies, and Cubs. I wasn't around the players' wives because I lived in Glenside. Being with the wives made you close to the team and I missed the camaraderie a lot. I did become good friends with Thurmon Munson's wife, however, because during the second spring training we sat around at the pool together. I was so saddened when her husband was killed in a plane crash. He had a marvelous career going before his untimely tragedy.

One of my most memorable moments of Johnny as a Yankee player took place while I was crossing the George Washington Bridge entering the Bronx. I attended many games while Johnny played in New York. I recall my friend Dottie and I crossing the bridge when we heard a horn honking. We had two cars at the time: Johnny had a love, a GTO with a 455 engine. He always loved fast cars, this one donned with the license plate JC 6. I was riding in our family station wagon labelled JWC 6. Not that we were sloganeering, crazy-type people, but I guess this is as far as Johnny got to braggadocio. At any rate, there was a group of young people trying to get my attention as we crossed the bridge. Traffic was heavy, as usual, and they pulled along side of us. "Hey! Are you Johnny Callison's wife?"

I said, "Yeah!"

"I thought so!" one of them yelled. "We're going to see him play today—wish he was still with the Phillies! Number 25, huh?" he queried!

As they passed, I felt very proud of Johnny and of being his wife. Number 25! I thought! He was number 9 with the White Sox—his hero's number, Ted Williams. He was number 6 with the Phillies and the Cubs—his other hero's number, Stan Musial. Other than number 25, he had some great numbers. Williams and Musial both batted left and threw right! Just a thought. They were great and so was Johnny.

*   *   *

206

John Sletten:

In August of 1959, Dad took me to a game at Yankee Stadium. We were on a family vacation visiting my parents' army-air corps friends from World War II. Needless to say, it was the biggest thrill of my life at that point. Dad's friend was a pilot with Air France and acquired first row seats at first base. The Yankees were playing the Boston Red Sox, and there I was sitting in the front row, on the field, watching my childhood heroes, Skowron, Mantle, Berra, Ford, Malzone, Jensen, and, of course, Ted Williams pass by. I was awestruck observing that magnificent structure. Previously I only pictured Yankee Stadium in my mind as listened to the World Series on the radio during the fifties. I wasn't disappointed!

I think the Red Sox won the game that day. I must have been too overwhelmed with being there and seeing the players to remember. I know for sure that Ted Williams and Mickey Mantle both hit home runs that day. But just being there was more than enough for me! I knew my friends back home would never believe that'd I'd actually been there.

After the game Dad and I took a walk out to the center-field fence to see the monuments. En route, I reached down to feel the grass. I pulled out a few strands and put them in my pocket while thinking about all my heroes who had once roamed the grounds.

As we walked, Dad pointed things out and told me a few stories. "This is Yankee Stadium, John, 'The House That Ruth Built'! " he said. "It was first dedicated in 1923. Before that the Yankees played across the river at the Giants' Polo Grounds. Then, about 1921, when Ruth started belting all those home runs, the Yankees started outdrawing the Giants four to one. John McGraw, the Giants' manager, told his owner, Horace Stoneham, that he better get the Yankees out of the Polo Grounds because it was becoming embarrassing. The eviction notice was delivered that day, and the Yankees bought this spot from William Waldorf Astor for $600,000. Look at the foul lines. The Yankees always had great left-handed hitters—see it is 296 in right, 301 in left, 461 out here where we're going in center. Babe Ruth hit the first home run ever here. It figures, doesn't it John?"

It would be redundant to recount any of the stories that Dad told me that day because anyone who'd be reading this baseball biography would have heard them all. It would be just as purposeless to describe the stadium for the same reason. It is the most well known of them all. But on that day in 1959, as we exited the ballpark between 157th and 161st at River Avenue, I remember looking back. I turned and just stared at the ballpark for five minutes or so. Inscribed on the edifice right before me it said, sure enough, THE HOUSE THAT RUTH BUILT.

*   *   *

I feel fortunate to have played in the old Yankee Stadium. It was just the way it was when Ruth played there. I often wondered during the 1972 season how many homers I would have hit had I played all my years in that stadium with the short right-field porch. Especially, the way I pulled the ball when I first came up. I'll never know, but I surely enjoyed my stint with the Yankees. They were a class organization, like the White Sox, and it was a good place to finish up. Dianne will never forget, one day, when there was a knock on the door at our home in Glenside and a florist greeted her. I had won the game that day in New York and the Yankees had sent her a bouquet of flowers. No other team had ever made a gesture like that before. I didn't know, of course, before the season began it would be my last; 1973 was the last year of old Yankee Stadium as well. After the season they closed it down for two years to make a $100 million face-lift.

Before the 1973 season began, my buddy Dick Allen signed a three-year contract with the Chicago White Sox for a record-breaking $250,000 per year. It was the highest salary in the history of the game. Additionally, the Player's Association successfully negotiated a deal whereby there would be an arbitrator sent in for salary disputes. The decision of the arbitrator, based on the facts, was binding. Good for the new guys—once again I just missed. They also came up with the "ten and five rule," whereby if a player had played ten years of major league ball, the last five with the same team, a player could veto a trade. These provisions gave veteran players new protection and autonomy.

Baseball was changing quickly. The American League broke with the National League by instituting the use of the designated hitter (DH). The purpose of this was to liven up the game by getting the pitchers out of the batting order, but more so, I thought, it was to give some of the older players, who couldn't play the field that well anymore but could still hit, a chance to prolong their careers. It seemed at the time a good thing for someone like me! With all this the 1973 campaign began.

It would be another historical season which would see Henry Aaron come within one home run of Babe Ruth's lifetime record, Nolan Ryan go beyond Sandy Koufax's single-season strikeout record, and the American League offer a rule which dramatically changed the style of play in the American League with the DH. Willie Mays, after twenty-one years in the Big Show, said good-bye to the game, playing only sixty-six games with the Mets as a result of injuries and age. I played thirty-two games in the outfield and ten games as a DH for the Yankees before I was told by Ralph Houk in Arlington, Texas, that my services were no longer needed.

I guess everyone who makes it to major league baseball figures they will play the game forever or time won't pass as quickly as it does. I played nearly sixteen years in the Bigs and now it was my time. In 1973 George Steinbrenner acquired the controlling financial interest of the Yankees, and I guess he didn't like what he saw. To this day he still doesn't, as history has certainly proved.

On August 18, 1973, we were in Arlington, Texas, for a weekend series with the Texas Rangers. Ralph Houk called me in his office, and when I saw tears in his eyes I knew I was in trouble.

"Johnny," he said. "I have to let you go! Steinbrenner wants to get rid of the veterans."

Seeing how badly he was taking it, I couldn't think of anything to say but, "When it's over, it's over!"

Ralph Houk was one of the finest human beings I've ever met. I was fortunate to play for good managers, save Leo perhaps, but I must say that Ralph was probably the best. He was definitely the best manager I ever saw in handling the players, especially pitchers. He worried about everyone on the club. He made each of us feel a part of the team whether playing regularly or not. He never knocked a player. Sometimes I almost thought he was too good. I often thought maybe he should rip some of us once in a while. He tried to satisfy everyone's needs on the club. He just had a way of getting the most out of his ballplayers, which is what managing's all about. And he certainly gave me a shot with the Yankees. However, in 1973 I just didn't have the legs anymore. In the forty-five games I played, I hit poorly, with a meager batting average of .176, one homer and ten RBIs. I was only thirty-four years old but felt fifty emotionally and physically. I didn't expect it to end this way, but nothing usually ends the way you think it might. The one thing I knew for sure—it was over! I just knew it right then.

*   *   *

John Sletten:

In 1973 I was conducting my accounting practice in Portsmouth, Virginia. I was still an avid baseball fan, and I remember the release of Johnny Callison. One always follows his stars, and Johnny was one of mine! I was saddened when he was released by the Yankees, but I thought for sure he would get picked up by another team. It didn't happen, and baseball went on.

I remember the 1973 season vividly. The Oakland A's and Cincinnati Reds appeared to becoming dynasties. But lo and behold, the crazy New York Mets, with incredible pitching, stole the Eastern Division and entered the National League championship series with a lowly record of 82–79. The powerful "Big Red Machine" won ninety-nine games. This was when the Mets' Tug McGraw coined the phrase "You gotta believe." The Mets took the Reds three of five, much to the protest of Pete Rose, who proclaimed the Mets didn't even have the right to play against them. The A's won the World Series, but it took them seven games to beat this second coming of the boys from Flushing.

Dick Allen, now baseball's highest-paid player, broke his leg during midseason and sat out the rest of the year. During the Series, Charley Finley, dismayed when a reserve second baseman named Mike Andrews committed two errors to give the Mets a victory, placed him on the disabled list. Dick Williams, manager of the A's, as a result, for his owner's interference, resigned at the end of the season. It was the beginning of the end for the A's! It was also the beginning of better days ahead for the players!

The year 1973 started out with the Miami Dolphins winning Super Bowl VII 14–7 over the Washington Redskins. On paper at least, the fighting stopped in Vietnam. George Foreman beat Joe Frazier for the heavyweight championship. And all of America was watching the Archie Bunkers.

Former President Lyndon Baines Johnson died on January 22, 1973. By April, Haldeman, chief of staff, and Erlichman, domestic adviser, had resigned over Watergate. The *Washington Post's* Woodward and Bernstein's investigative journalism set the Senate panel to begin the Watergate hearings. In June, John Dean, White House counsel, accused Nixon and his two chief aides, Haldeman and Erlichman, in the Watergate cover-up. Meanwhile sinewy racehorse Secretariat won the Triple Crown at the Belmont Stakes.

In October, Vice President Agnew resigned in disgrace and was replaced by Congressman Gerry Ford of Michigan. By year end Nixon announced an oil shortage, and the Empire State Building was replaced by the World Trade Center as the highest structure in New York. In the movies, Newman and Redford starred in *The Sting*. And Streisand and Redford made us all think back to a less complicated past in *The Way We Were*.

Chapter Nine

Life without Baseball

Once I wrote down on the empty spaces of a timetable the names of those who came to Gatsby's house that summer. It is an old timetable now, disintegrating at its folds. . . . But I can still read the gray names, and they will give you a better impression than my generalities of those who accepted Gatsby's hospitality and paid him the subtle tribute of knowing nothing whatever about him. . . . Everyone suspects himself of at least one of the cardinal virtues, and this is mine: I am one of the few honest people that I have ever known.

—F. Scott Fitzgerald, *The Great Gatsby*

Frankly, I was so young when I started I never thought about life without baseball. In my latter years I watched some of the older stars leaving the game, but I still felt my time was way off. Actually, it ended as quickly as it began. In retrospect, it was probably easier that way, because there was no time to think.

Mostly, I missed my friends in baseball. I didn't miss playing the game. When your knees go south—that's it! Emotionally, though, leaving the game was very difficult. I'd been in professional baseball for eighteen years—sixteen of them in the Bigs. I was just thirty-four years old when I hung it up. What is tough is knowing you're a celebrity one day, people patting you on the back and requesting an autograph, and the following day you're nobody. Worse yet, there was not much demand for me in the nine-to-five

213

world. I was trained to hit a major league curveball and fastball. Now I found myself in the real world trying to compete against kids with college degrees or older fellows who had years of experience in their field. Believe me, yesterday's hero is not exactly a hot item, and fans have this crazy idea that ball players just retire to sit around a hot fire, reliving their careers and anticipating invitations to old-timers' games. But it doesn't work that way. Rather, I found myself asking the same question a fifteen year old might ask: What am I going to do when I grow up? That is a helluva frightening position to be in at age thirty-four, and burying your head in old scrapbooks only makes it worse.

Perhaps I was ready! Ready to leave baseball but not ready to face a new and uncertain future. When I was at the top of my career there were a lot of people who told me to contact them when playing days were through. But too much time had passed and people forget. Also, I was no Joe Namath or Bob Uecker. I couldn't wear panty hose on television, nor could I capitalize on being a lousy major leaguer, because I wasn't. I respect Joe Namath and Bob Uecker very much, but I left show business when I took off the baseball uniform.

I guess, in retrospect, I took the end of my baseball career badly. I knew it was over as a player, but I really thought I'd be a part of the game forever. Dianne kept telling me I'd be picked up by some team as a player at first. I even made a few calls and everyone was really kind, but not interested. My best shot was with the Phillies, but when Phils manager Danny Ozark said no—that was it! So it was finally over and I had to get on with my life.

But I couldn't! All the people I thought would be there now were stammering and embarrassed. They had nothing to offer. I fooled with playing exhibition baseball games for Jenkintown Steel, but no job materialized. I tried selling electronics, cars, and other shit. I found out quickly I was no salesman!

I accepted a salesman position with Broadway Chrysler-Plymouth. This turned out to be a joke. Customers would come in and I would field baseball questions, sign autographs, etc., while other salesmen wrote up the deals. I was used, made no money, and became very pissed off. I went to work for the Nautilus gym for a while and made no money, but as least I got to work out. Then, finally, I went to work for Avis. Here, I had a chance. I stayed for nearly five years. One car, one price—nobody got screwed and I felt no pressure. It was a good deal for people buying those cars, and I felt comfortable.

But more than anything, I wanted to get back into baseball and I decided to call the Phillies. Hell, I was willing to work as a coach, a batting instructor, a front office aide, or even a season ticket salesman. However, the Phillies politely informed me that there were no openings and wished me good luck. I mean, I thought I was a pretty big name for the Phillies at one time, but professional sports is a cold, cold business. Once you're out—you're out! So, I settled into the car business, which beat going door to door selling pots and pans or some equivalent.

The boss suggested that I hang some baseball memorabilia on the walls in my office, and the guys I worked with soon called it my "Wall of Fame." I'll never forget one afternoon when business was slow I looked at the back of one of my baseball cards and realized my whole life's history was on a bubble gum card. In a way that saddened me, but my "Wall of Fame" was good for business.

Customers observed the "gallery" and would recall a catch I had made or a homer I'd hit. I was amazed how many people recognized me—mostly by name. Most of them asked the same question though: "What are you doing here?" They couldn't understand why a big shot like me would be selling cars. I told them I owned the place and sent them home feeling better.

All of this was in 1976. Reggie Jackson now played the same position I had played for the Yankees in 1973. Then, I made $40,000; Reggie had signed for $3,000,000. Good for him, but it didn't seem fair. It still doesn't!

I didn't like all the bouncing around between teams toward the end of my career; in fact, that's when you know you're at the end of the line. I began looking for something else to get into, but what? I thought about a restaurant, but other players had attempted this dream and lost their asses. I lost mine in another way! A friend of mine told me to invest in stocks, but every stock in which I invested went down the tubes. That's the great thing about the long term contracts today's players sign. They have security money up front! When I was playing no one signed for more than one year. For instance, whenever John Quinn and I negotiated a contract I'd physically throw up. It wasn't a negotiation! Rather, it was a scolding, and I was lucky if he didn't cut my pay. I would tell him what I wanted, and he'd just sit there with a laughing smirk on his face. "You're nuts," he would say. "I've been trying to trade you, but no team wants you. Either sign for what I'm offering or I'll release you." I'd curse under my breath, but I knew he would release me if I didn't sign. He always acted as though he was handing me over the deed to his home.

During a moment of nostalgia, Dianne convinced me to drive to 21st and Lehigh the day before they began tearing down Connie Mack Stadium. As we drove by the old ballpark, Dianne began to cry, remembering all of the great games. You know what I thought about? John Quinn, that old asshole, sitting up in that dingy old office—yeah that's right, guarding the safe!

Time passed and our investments were soon gone. We were barely making it, when Dianne went to work as a waitress at the Holiday Inn in Fort Washington. She went to work at five in the morning (hell, she never went to bed until then in the old days) and worked until 3:00 P.M. The kids were in school, but when they got home she was there as usual. I can't tell you how I admired her. She'd never worked a job in her life, but when the chips were down she went right after it for us.

I guess the worst times were around the mid-seventies—probably 1976. You find out quickly who your friends are! You try to be proud people, and I guess we've always been that. But what got us through were our friends. Really, really good friends.

At age forty-five (1984) the baseball pension kicked in. Finally, I felt some relief. All of the hard work was about to pay off in some kind of way, and I could feel somewhat respectable once again.

I give a lot of credit to my fellow players. We helped mold the future for today's players. We're also doing something now for the guys who fall on bad times after their playing days are over. Again, no one is prouder than an athlete! I never thought of asking for financial help, but today a player can do just that. We came close to losing our home. We have friends and teammates that have lost everything. Former great players, like Early Wynn, lead organizations now that help the ballplayers that have it bad after baseball. It's difficult for anyone to ask for help; I never did, but maybe I would have if they had what they got going now. There are widow's funds, hard-timer's situation funds, and lots of other good things. The players from my generation set up all of this and I'm proud of it. I think we were a great generation of players. We didn't get paid well, at least if you consider what a ballplayer makes today, but our efforts have made it better for everyone who's ever been there, is now, or might be.

In the back of my mind I thought there was the possibility that the Phillies might offer me a job once my playing days were done. Maybe they would have if I'd pursued it, but I didn't, and they tendered no offers. I had some of the great hitters of all time teach me batting techniques and I think I could have passed some of my knowledge onto the youth coming up, but no one else was thinking along those lines evidently. On the other hand, most jobs for former players begin in the minor leagues, and I had no interest in traveling or moving around. Plus the pay stunk—it did then, anyway. I always thought it strange that a ball club will make a million-dollar investment in a young player, and look for a coach that will accept a $5,000 salary. It's improved today, but back in my era that was the situation. My friend and teammate Jim Bunning went to the minors to coach and eventually managed a club. He is such an aggressive-type guy and, of course, wanted to manage in the majors. However, his personality dictated a policy that commanded, "my way, or the highway," and that just doesn't work in baseball politics. Jim is doing well now, though, as a U.S. congressman from the state of Kentucky. He even ran for governor of that state a few years ago.

We had some very bad years after baseball, but we somehow worked our way through. As the years passed, baseball and I grew further apart. I never went to a game and rarely listened to one on the radio or watched TV. I'm not really sure why. I had a good career but felt left out in the cold when my playing days ended. Simply, the clubs just don't care! Once you're done as a player, they're finished with you! It's very difficult to accept.

I've been asked by almost everyone the reason I left the game at such a young age. Actually, I couldn't run anymore. I started playing professionally at eighteen, and my last year with the Yankees I was really run-down. In fact, the last five years of my career I taped my knees before every game. At the end, my neck ached and I felt simply out of gas. For example, as a younger player I was always looking for that extra base. My last season I remember hitting a single, and the next batter hit a gapper, forcing me to run from first to third. It damned near killed me and I began to really realize that it was about over. *No more gappers*, I used to pray when I was on base. A few years prior I had watched Roy Sievers in the twilight of his career. I'll never forget Roy trying to get an inside-the-park home run, and watching him, literally, crawl across home plate. The look on his face was scary—I thought he was going to die.

So, in the beginning it was kind of a relief getting released. Besides aching physically, I wasn't enjoying the game emotionally anymore as well. When you aren't playing regularly and you're older, your body tightens up. You become bored sitting in the dugout, which in turn makes it difficult to concentrate on the game.

During the last two years of my career I learned to appreciate the tough role of a pinch hitter. It's the hardest job in baseball. You get put into games in clutch situations. You're not loose. You're put into the game and your timing is way off because you haven't hit maybe for a day or two. I don't remember what I hit for average as a pinch hitter, but I do remember winning seven or eight games for the Yankees in that capacity. It is a very tough role to fill!

Looking back, I'd do it all over again. I worked at the game and gave 100 percent most of the time. The nature of the business is very uncertain. Even though you have ability, you go into slumps and you're pressured to perform. Every player is aware that eventually there will be that day in the near or distant future when their athletic ability will be gone. So, in final analysis, I suppose I was fortunate to have had a lengthy career. Life after baseball was very disappointing and upsetting, but I would have never given up the baseball.

Today life is better. Somehow it all worked out! I've had wonderful support from friends, family, and especially my wife. Our three daughters live nearby, and we enjoy our grandchildren very much. Lori has two daughters, Jessica (9) and Juli (7). Cindy has three daughters, Ashlee (9), Nicole (6), and Courtney, born February 22, 1991. Sherri has three daughters, Jamie (6), Lindsay (5), and Brittany (1).

About the game and players today? Every generation probably claims their time was the best. But I still think baseball had its top caliber of teams back in the fifties and the sixties when there were only eight teams in each league. It just stands to reason! Perhaps there are some better athletes today because the kids seem to be bigger and stronger, but our teams were better. I truly believe that we had a better game back then.

The players and their big money? I'm for them getting as much money as they can. More power to them! I certainly feel badly that I missed out on the big money, but that's the way it worked out—I was born too early. The only thing I don't understand about the players today is their feelings toward the old-timers. When I came up, I felt playing on the same field with Ted Williams was like being in the presence of God. We treated all the former stars with such reverence. Today, it seems like the young guys don't even knew we exist or existed. Too bad for them!

The year 1983 saw the Philadelphia Phillies celebrate their 100th-year anniversary. They had a campaign with the fans to vote for the most outstanding Phillies players during the tenure of the ball club. I was proud to have the fans vote me to one of the outfield positions for the all-time Phillies team. Each one of us had our special night at Veterans Stadium. Mine was July 3rd. A lot of our friends were in the ballpark that night, including our children. Dianne was with me as they introduced me that night. It was a thrill and an honor!

Dianne and the family surprised me with a party at the Sheraton in Fort Washington after the game. She even played the old White Sox movie they made of me when I first started out. During the running of the film, I couldn't help but reminisce about that first at bat in Commiskey Park. Then, for a fleeting moment, thinking of my biggest disappointment—being traded by the Sox. I thought about facing the best pitcher I ever faced—Sandy Koufax. My final thought was about the biggest thrill of all—a Dick Radatz fastball I deposited in the right-field pavilion at Shea Stadium to win the 1964 all-star game for the National League.

*   *   *

Sherri Callison Curran:

I remember being at the shore when my dad retired. He came there and told my mom it was over. I didn't understand at the time, but it was the beginning of changes.

I don't remember much about the baseball. I recall getting our books and clothes together to travel to spring training. This was fun! It was a time to go swimming, fishing, and be with Dad.

My recollections are few. I remember Joe Pepitone curling his hair. I recall riding on the bus with the team. When Dad was with the Yankees some of the boys in school used to tease me, saying things like, "Your dad strikes out all of the time."

Today is different! I'll be at a party and someone will always introduce me as Johnny Callison's daughter. They'll respond: "Hey, your dad was a great hitter. He was a great right fielder." I'm always proud!

I'm not a sports fan to this day. But I do remember being at Dad's games. I would just walk around the stadium purchasing hot dogs and talking to the security guards.

Now that I'm older, I understand more what my dad was all about. I'm really proud of him. But he'll always be just Dad to me. And he is a good dad!

*   *   *

Dianne Callison:

I went to the shore with my neighbor Dottie the day after Johnny left on his road trip to Texas. I was lying on the beach when Dottie came up to me, saying, "I hate to give you this but I think you should read it!" The paper said: "John Callison released by Yanks." I was distraught. All I could do was cry. I felt so sorry for Johnny and worried about how he was feeling and where he was at that moment. He couldn't reach me because he wasn't aware I had decided to go to the South Jersey shore. I wasn't even sure where the team was staying in Arlington, but I guessed correctly and reached Johnny just before he was leaving for the airport. He told me he was flying directly to Philly, and I told him that I would meet him there.

I was devastated. But I didn't feel it was over. I thought for sure Johnny would pick up with another team, if not for the rest of the season, certainly by spring training. I was amazed when it didn't happen, and the following winter was the longest one we ever spent. For sixteen years we had been spending our winters in the South. That year we spent our first winter in Pennsylvania. It was the strangest feeling, but the fact that it was over finally settled.

Before Johnny's release, baseball had already changed a lot for me. We had spent the summers with him for two years in Chicago, but when he went with the Yankees he chose to commute. He didn't want to live in New York, and the children were settled in school. Therefore, I didn't feel as much a part of the team as I did in Philadelphia and even Chicago. It was different—certainly wasn't as exciting. When he played in New York I would drive up for a lot of games and still flew to nearby cities to be with him when he was on the road. But it was different, the girls were getting older, and I guess baseball was winding down for us. I just didn't want to think about it! Now, I had to.

Life after baseball was rough—especially at first. Johnny didn't know what to do. Not only was he rejected by other teams in both leagues to continue his career—so-called friends didn't fulfill commitments in job opportunities. After various attempts at a variety of jobs, he finally settled with selling cars for Avis for five years. I started waitressing, and between the two of us, we managed to keep our home—everything else was gone.

Through it all Johnny never complained, and I guess I didn't either—that's just the way we are. But it took its toll on Johnny, as he harbors everything inside of him. In 1986 Johnny decided to have a stress test. He complained of chest pains and would find himself breathless just carrying trash cans from the street. His ulcers had been acting up for three or four years, and just two days before he was to go in for his heart testing, he began hemorrhaging and throwing up blood. He was rushed to the hospital, where the doctors were successful getting the hemorrhaging stopped, but it recurred again twenty-four hours later. The decision was made to remove half of his stomach, and while he was in intensive care, following the surgery, he had a heart attack. Six weeks later, the doctors performed five bypasses. Thank God, Johnny recovered and looks great today!

People ask me the same question. Was your life in baseball worth it? My answer is always, "I wouldn't trade it for anything." The glory years were terrific. The disappointments are perhaps no more than most people suffer who are not in the limelight. The traveling was difficult—going cross country by myself with the children crying and fighting, dogs barking, etc. But we all experienced a lot and baseball life was good. I can probably put it best by saying, for all we went through being baseball people, and for the financial misery of a few years after—even to the extent of seeing Johnny sic the dog after the water department man who was there to cut our water off—we had our Camelot! And I like to say ours was for more than one brief shining moment.

References

Golenbock, Peter. *Bums: An Oral History of the Brooklyn Dodgers.*
New York: Pocket Books, 1986.
Neft, David S. and Richard M. Cohen. *The Sports Encyclopedia:
Baseball.* 9th ed. New York: St. Martin's Press, 1989.
Reidenbaugh, Lowell. *Take Me Out to the Ball Park.* Rev. 2d ed. St.
Louis, Missouri: The Sporting New Publishing Co., 1989.
Chronicle of the 20th Century. Mount Kisco, New York: Chronicle Pub-
lications, Inc. Conceived and published by Jacques Legrand, 1987.